Froebel and Social Justice

FROEBEL IN PRACTICE

Series Editors: Sacha Powell and Tina Bruce

A series of short and accessible guides to the Froebelian approach in Early Childhood Education and Care, written by Froebel-trained practicing educators and scholars, in partnership with the Froebel Trust. Each book in the series emphasizes a different focus of the Froebelian principles. Informed by the latest research the books offer suggestions for practice around topics such as unity and connectedness, autonomous learning, valuing childhood in its own right, relationships matter, creativity and the power of symbols, the central importance of play, engaging with nature, knowledgeable and nurturing educators.

Forthcoming in the series:

Froebel, Literacy and Mathematics, Jane Whinnett

Froebel and Social Justice

RACHNA JOSHI

BLOOMSBURY ACADEMIC
LONDON • NEW YORK • OXFORD • NEW DELHI • SYDNEY

BLOOMSBURY ACADEMIC
Bloomsbury Publishing Plc, 50 Bedford Square, London, WC1B 3DP, UK
Bloomsbury Publishing Inc, 1385 Broadway, New York, NY 10018, USA
Bloomsbury Publishing Ireland, 29 Earlsfort Terrace, Dublin 2,
D02 AY28, Ireland

BLOOMSBURY, BLOOMSBURY ACADEMIC and the Diana logo are trademarks of Bloomsbury Publishing Plc

First published in Great Britain 2026

Cover image by D Purohit of Arjun Khevan

A catalogue record for this book is available from the British Library.

A catalog record for this book is available from the Library of Congress.

ISBN: HB: 978-1-3505-2933-5
PB: 978-1-3505-2932-8
ePDF: 978-1-3505-2935-9
eBook: 978-1-3505-2934-2

Series: Froebel in Practice

Typeset by Newgen KnowledgeWorks Pvt. Ltd., Chennai, India
Printed and bound in Great Britain

For product safety related questions contact productsafety@bloomsbury.com.

To find out more about our authors and books visit www.bloomsbury.com and sign up for our newsletters.

This book is dedicated to the children of Gaza, and all children whose strength shines brightly in the face of injustice, and their educators who courageously and compassionately strive to create meaningful change in their communities.

CONTENTS

FIGURES

TABLE

SERIES EDITORS' FOREWORD

By

Dr Sacha Powell,

Series Co-Editor, Chief Executive Officer, The Froebel Trust.

When Mark Richardson, Senior Commissioning Editor for Bloomsbury suggested a partnership with the Froebel Trust for a short-form book series it made perfect sense!

Interest has escalated in the pedagogy for early childhood education, which Friedrich Froebel (1782–1852) constructed philosophically and exemplified in the practices he adopted with young children within his Kindergarten. More educators are finding themselves drawn to the underpinning principles that respect children's lives and learning and resist technocratic educational practices.

With leading Froebel scholar and educator Professor Tina Bruce at the helm of this collaboration – as co-editor of the series and mentor to the authors – Bloomsbury's relationship with the international Froebelian community continues to grow in strength while enabling new voices to make original contributions to the field of research-informed guidance for early childhood educators.

We welcome you to the 'Froebel in Practice' series.

In a field as dynamic and vital as early childhood education, professionals may find themselves seeking tangible advice to help navigate our complex social world and philosophical landscapes. Academic texts provide essential theoretical grounding, yet the challenge remains: *How do we translate these profound ideas into the immediate, lived experience of a child in a modern early learning and childcare setting?*

This is the gap our short-form book series aims to bridge – helping educators to dig even deeper than the very popular Froebelian Approach pamphlets that are freely published on the Froebel Trust's website.[1] Believing in the importance of widespread, equitable rights to read high quality scholarship and practice guidance, the trustees of the Froebel Trust set aside funds to cover the Open Access fees for this series of books.

Our intention with 'Froebel in Practice' is to offer busy educators – whether they are new trainees or experienced professionals – a reservoir of accessible, practical and highly focused guides. The complex, holistic philosophy of Friedrich Froebel is transformed into manageable, actionable elements, ensuring his timeless principles remain connected, relevant and vibrant today. Each volume in this series shows how this framework of principles keeps Froebelian pedagogy dynamic and responsive to its context, ensuring contemporary relevance without loss of integrity.

Each author addresses a timely – some might say urgent – topic: becoming literate in its broadest sense; experiencing and advocating social justice; and embracing inclusion. By focusing intensely on application, we move beyond mere description, showing *what* high-quality, play-based education looks like in real-world scenarios.

We fundamentally believe that theory must inform practice, and practice must illuminate theory. This series is designed to nurture and sustain critically reflective practice, providing specific examples that educators can immediately discuss and refine within their own teams. Furthermore, these books help educators explicitly to connect their deep, relationship-based

[1]To view or download the Froebelian Approach pamphlet series, please go online to: https://www.froebel.org.uk/training-and-resources/pamphlets.

work to contemporary educational frameworks or curricula, empowering them to articulate the profound value of a Froebelian approach.

Drawing on the wisdom of expert educators and the latest research facilitated by the Froebel Trust and others, these books offer credible, experience-informed advice.

By engaging with 'Froebel in Practice', educators will be empowered to create environments where babies and children are inspired and supported to learn how to learn – developing autonomy, expressing creativity, and exhibiting self-motivation. Our hope is that this series makes Froebel's enduring vision less abstract and more readily achievable, supporting exceptional early childhood education for every baby and child.

ACKNOWLEDGEMENTS

I am hugely grateful to Sacha Powell, the Froebel Trust and Bloomsbury for commissioning this series. Thank you to my fellow Froebelians and the Travelling Tutor team for deep discussions and inspirations.

To my family and friends, thank you for your encouragement and unconditional love. It has been a constant source of strength.

A special thanks to Sayeed for his photo editing and unwavering support through this book writing journey.

Writing this book has been a learning curve from start to finish, I am especially thankful to Tina Bruce for all her encouragement, patience and guidance throughout the process.

I hope this book ignites conversations and sparks debate about our current state and renews commitment towards social justice.

CHAPTER 1

Introduction

Social justice affects all of our thoughts and actions every day. It is a deeply embedded and structural issue that ingrains itself into the lives of individuals in the past, present and future. There are events which highlight continual injustice within political systems, governmental structures, communities and everyday interactions. Experiencing and witnessing this brings about mistrust and fragmentation between others and the institutions that claim to support those within them. The inequality that many people face creates a sentiment of despair and division. Those who are looking to examine their practices and work towards social justice venture into this arena with trepidation.

This book aims to explore the themes within social justice through a Froebelian philosophical framework. Froebelian education is holistic and connected by a network of thinking that originates from before the nineteenth century and continues today. Not only are Froebel's ideas later confirmed by contemporary academic research, these ideas are embodied by educators who engage with evolving dialogues and discussions linking theory, practice, policy and politics together.

Having a critical consciousness or 'conscientization' as described by Freire (1970, 1994, 1998) is the process of continually questioning, reflecting and acting on ideas within the social consciousness. This includes critiquing daily practice in educational contexts to government policies and frameworks. Freirean and Froebelian education complement each other (Tang and Rubiano, 2025).

Froebel's idea of life unification, unity and connectedness, with Freire's praxis aid to the exploration of social justice within education today. During Froebel's life he advocated for women's role in education. This was regarded as revolutionary thinking and ridiculed by others; '"Does Herr Froebel mean we shall eventually have women university professors?" – the minutes of one assembly record that delegates erupted in hilarious laughter' (Liebschner, 1992: 28). Froebel took collective action through empowering educators, children and the community by addressing socially unjust practices. Similarly, Freire describes the role of education to be 'rooted in the ethical formation both of selves and of history' describing the entanglement with contemporary voices and influences creating an ever-changing dynamic (Freire, 1998: 23; Sakr and Kaur, 2024).

Building on these frameworks, the four freedoms provide an additional layer to draw on (Roosevelt, 2012; Roosevelt, 1941). These formed the foundations of the Universal Declaration of Human Rights (FDR library, n.d.; United Nations, 1948). These and other legislations or policies are discussed but not without critique.

This work situates itself in a decolonial epistemology interrogating the intersection between colonialism and its impact on education across the globe (Mignolo, 2012). Through this there is an acknowledgement of the entanglement between indigenous people and practices and the Western frameworks used that determines what social justice might look like in early childhood education. These include the Universal Declaration of Human Rights (UDHR) and the United Nations Convention of the Rights of the Child (UCRC). More contemporary goals include the Sustainable Development Goals (SDGs) upheld by the three pillars of sustainability (United Nations, 2015). These incorporate environmental, social and economic factors into the work of social justice. The Eurocentric positionality is not overlooked when it comes to interrogating the use of these constitutions and goals with intentional cross examination to ensure a wider perspective is pursued.

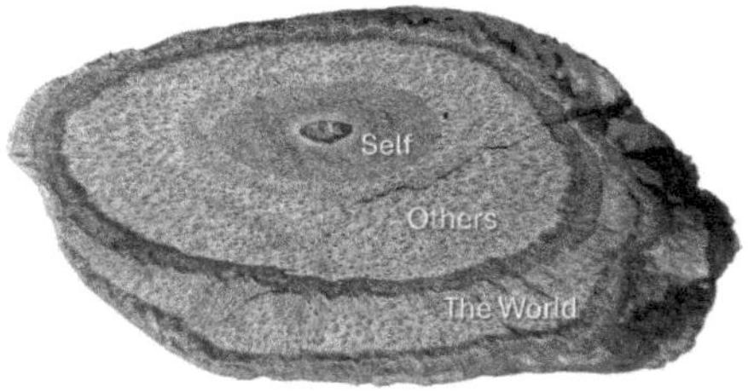

FIGURE 1.1 Froebelian framework of self, others and world. Adapted from Joshi (2023).

The chapters are organized in a Froebelian framework – starting with the 'self' as illustrated in Figure 1.1. Chapter 2 explores Identity and promotes the self-reflection of educators and how they can support children's developing sense of self. Widening out to 'others', Chapter 3, Diversity, looks at the communal aspect of social justice, celebrating and accepting similarities and differences. Moving to the 'world', Chapters 4 and 5, Equality and Equity, explore the topics conceptually, through both idealistic and realistic perspectives. The freedoms: from fear, want, of speech, worship are explored in Chapters 6, 7, 8 and 9. Each chapter takes a deep dive into a freedom examining how it emerges in early childhood education and ways to counter and respond. Chapter 10 summarizes how educators need to ensure access and support active participation to work towards social justice.

Language and terminology

There has been research ensuring appropriate terminology throughout the book but language evolves and meanings can change. Examples provide context to themes and issues arising. The children, families and educators have been anonymized to protect their identity. Children's ages are included within the examples. The term 'family' is used to describe a broad version of family, which might include relatives, family-friends, kinship carers and so on (Williams and Joshi, 2025).

Social justice in early childhood education

A socially just system envisions an eradication of unnecessary suffering, tyranny, oppression, prejudice and discrimination becoming a reality (Jost and Kay, 2010). Early childhood education is an important place to start this process: 'Early childhood care and education is the most transformative investment a country can make to give all children a fair start in life and combat inequalities early on' (United Nations Educational Scientific Cultural Organization and United Nations Children's Fund, 2024).

When educators work together, it helps to widen the narrow individualistic viewpoints and encourages reflection from each individual in how they can commit and contribute to a collective whole and imagine a fair society for today.

This book examines what it means to be socially just, embedding the goals of equity, equality, inclusion and diversity into practice and how these themes can be applied through a Froebelian educational lens (Social Justice Collective, n.d.).

CHAPTER 2

Identity

Understanding and exploring identity is a subject that has been debated and discussed for millennia, yet is still relevant and complex today. The philosophical approaches that try to understand the 'essence of self' are based in a variety of historic and cultural contexts. Asian philosophies idealize the realization of the true self. European philosophy argued for the perfect form or idea. This later evolved into an entanglement of the Romantic and Enlightenment period where the focus shifted from identity being determined by divine will and instead towards the interrelation between autonomous individuals, nature and science (Beljan, 2025).

Today, identity has a people-centred approach highlighting the need for self-consciousness and self-recognition (Xu and Xie, 2021). However, Ghosh et al. (2008: 58) write 'In colonial relationships, identity may have assumed a more rigidified status, for based on the colonisers' needs, identity modification, at least in those situations, was not an environmentally induced social stimuli-response phenomenon, but was artificially produced and maintained for the promulgation as well as the perpetuation of the colonial agenda.' To redress this colonial perspective would be to understand the social and environmental constructs of identity formation.

Identity is helpfully understood as a social construct encompassing conscious and unconscious thoughts and feelings of the individual. The social realm which forms this sense of identity is not fixed and is instead fluid and dynamic suiting this socially just and decolonial lens. There are irrational and contradictory behaviours of individuals that develop into a complex identity that is constantly reinventing and shifting through negotiations with power and society (Guimarães, 2025; Robinson and Diaz, 2016). When educators work with children, their role in supporting the fluidity of children's developing sense of identity is hugely important. Froebel wrote about how 'education as a whole should bring a man to consciousness', he emphasized the role of education in leading children to clarity of their internal self, and the interrelationship with others, building on the principle of unity and connectedness (Froebel, 1826: 2; Froebel Trust, 2021). Finding similarities and celebrating differences are an essential part of Froebelian philosophy.

This chapter explores the concept of 'Who am I and who are you?' through the lens of educators, and their role in supporting children. It is underpinned with the understanding that both nurturing identity and a sense of self is an underlying action that promotes peaceful coexistence in society (Francis, 2021).

Autoethnography

Autoethnography suggests the researcher is the subject (Belbase et al., 2008). It matters to explore author bias and positionality. This refers to personal opinions, beliefs or values influenced by the multitude of identities that the author intersects. In every book, fiction or non-fiction, the author will bring a lens, viewpoint or an opinion which may be subconsciously or overtly integrated into the storytelling. Knowing and realizing this lens, recognizes how the professional and personal are intertwined. It implores readers to be critical of the content and to reflect on their own views and positionality.

The author of this book is an educator working in inner-city settings, concerned with addressing social justice causes and exploring a possible alignment of this work with Froebelian educational practice. Awareness of bias and subjectivity strengthens the effort to be as objective as possible. Freire (1998: 22) writes: 'I am not impartial or objective; not a fixed observer of facts and happenings ... Whoever really observes, does so from a given point of view'. Bourke (2014) adds that 'we can strive to remain objective, but must be ever mindful of our subjectivities'. This 'insider/outsider' perspective as described by Gregory and Ruby (2011) explains the feelings of those who find alignment with the side of the research*ed* but find themselves also on the side of the research*er.* By acknowledging the position one is in as writer, practitioner or researcher, there is a development of critical thinking and critical consciousness (Freire, 1970). Critical consciousness is underpinned by the interconnection of relationships and understanding of how one is 'situated' in the space. For example, the author being a member of the endorsed Froebel Trust travelling tutors group hugely influences the position taken. Understanding our own past events and experiences helps us to make sense of how our beliefs have shaped our thinking today (Tang and Rubiano, 2025). Freire (1998) warns not to become dogmatic of beliefs, instead emphasizing an ethical grounding or philosophy.

Exploring Froebel's ethnographical context aims to place his educational principles within a social justice framework. With the early death of his mother, and rejection from his father, Froebel's life was full of hardship. Through his maternal uncle he found care and nurture late in his childhood. In terms of his own self-reflection of his experience and identity he writes, 'I was not allowed to know myself in childish play' (Liebschner, 1992: 1). He demonstrates his acute awareness of what he was lacking in his childhood and his work in setting up schools and the Kindergarten created something that he himself would have benefitted from. Acts of social justice or resistance towards what is considered norm can be manifested on a personal scale through self-reflection, action and commitment (Furman, 2012). Froebel's writing evolved over time, demonstrating the praxis that Freire upholds (hooks, 1994). Froebel and Freire's writing was revolutionary, grounded by ethical positionality and embodied social justice (Tang et al., 2025).

Social identity and personal identity

It is necessary to look at the author's identity as this contextualizes the basis of the work. Examining one's sense of self can be challenging. There are personal and social identities which may be known, unknown and ever-changing (Tembo, 2024). A personal identity is what makes up the individual's values, perspectives and opinions. For children, their personal identity is typically influenced by their family life, first hand experiences and wider community. A social identity is based on the categories created by society and defined by the way people live. This can include physical attributes which can impact how society views an individual (Derman-Sparks et al., 2020). This might include nationality, heritage, gender, religion, race, neurotype and perceived body ability. The author's social identity would be, British Indian, Hindu, cis-woman, racialized as Brown, neurotypical and able-bodied. Personal and social identities interweave creating a unique sense of identity and belonging to certain groups, as well as inner values that are found within relationships.

There are cultural, situational parts that also make up a whole individual's personal identity (Ellemers et al., 2002). For example, the author's social identity includes being a professional who has attended further education and lives in her own home and working in an inner city. She has a family with two parents, and has made non-traditional choices about having children. Her immigration status, citizenship and residency have never been changed. Each of these can indicate various historical perspectives and circumstances, current thinking and values including socio-economic class, access to education, financial circumstances, personal choices, priorities and principles. All these aspects of an individual form the contexts in which they live. An individual would hold a combination of characteristics and values which can influence external perspectives of their identity.

These aspects of identity tell us part of a story; they draw up stereotypes and create assumptions. A certain individual or family experience may be common, such as divorce or moving home, but the experiences that the individual has means that each family will have their own stories, values and beliefs which impact on their way of thinking and being. Similarly, an individual's external characteristics do not show the intricacies and history of their experience. Assumptions about characteristics can lead to creating harmful viewpoints particularly in the context of children who are making sense of their identity. Baroness Lola Young (2024) who has Nigerian heritage, writes of her life with a white foster carer from babyhood and how the records from this early stage in her life show discrimination towards her physical descriptions. These have an impact on how children understand their identity, which is often seen through the lens of others.

Bias

Bias is the assumptions our brains make when prioritizing the millions of messages that are received. These can be based on relationships, categories and observations of the world around us. These help us to make sense of the world but also form unconscious or implicit bias (University of Washington Tacoma, 2015). If left unchecked these messages can lead to harmful stereotypes. Unravelling bias promotes understanding of where it comes from and how to counter it. Admitting bias, judgements or stereotypes can be difficult but are an important part of countering and addressing our behaviours through action and commitment towards social justice.

During a staff training session, the trainer shared this understanding of bias. An educator remarked, 'but we are early years educators – we don't have bias?' The altruistic sentiment of the profession leaves many individuals thinking they are exempt from unfair or unequal practice. Louis and Betteridge (2024) explain how all humans will make instinctive judgements based on what is seen, felt and heard. Therefore, all educators *will* have bias. By 'inspecting our actions and values' there is an accountability towards bias and ensuring that it is responded to (Conolly in Bruce, 1987: 149).

Types of bias include affinity bias where there is a preference towards others who share the same characteristic as ourselves. For example, a male educator who always favours the boys in the class. Confirmation bias is when there is an idea or belief and information is sought to only support it. For example, believing that all Asian children are academically gifted and foregrounding situations that confirm this. Attribution bias is when issues or errors are assigned to a child's character. For example, labelling a child as 'naughty' instead of considering whether their needs are being met (Louis and Betteridge, 2020). In order to see our biases educators must be self-reflective. This could be in the form of continual reflective questioning with colleagues, videoing practice, peer observations, utilizing toolkits and incorporated into regular supervision meetings.

An underpinning of deep, critical, honest self-reflection and action is foundational towards social justice. Starting with personal introspection provides a firm basis for working towards socially just praxis (Furman, 2012). For educators who are exploring their personal and social identities, the areas to reflect may be around: ethnicity or heritage, housing and immigration status, family structure, languages, racial identity, gender, sexuality, religious beliefs, age, education, health and economic class (Derman-Sparks et al., 2020). Exploring these aspects can raise complex feelings about oneself, particularly in relation to unwritten and unspoken expectations, positions and ideas within society.

Positionality of identity

The 'insider/outsider' perspective can be applied to the individual within society, who might feel that their identity aligns with some parts of society but are made to feel like an outsider in other aspects. These complex feelings need to be addressed and so confronting the idea of oneself being an 'insider' or an 'outsider' plays an important part in working towards social justice. For an individual being on the 'inside' of societal expectations, it may not seem obvious that they are living in an advantageous position, particularly when there may be disadvantages attributed to their identity too. Being in this position may come with an entitlement or a belief that others also hold their viewpoint, they may not understand or realize that what they have or have not experienced is based on their social identity. For example, a Black educator explained that he was late for work because he was stopped by the police. The white manager did not feel that this was a good-enough reason and did not understand why the police had stopped him if he had done nothing wrong. This entitlement viewpoint of the manager assumes that everyone has the same experiences with the police when in fact in 2023 statistics showed that it is five times more likely that a Black person is stopped by the police in the UK (National Statistics, 2024).

In contrast to the feeling of advantage, comes the feeling of disadvantage (or feeling like an outsider). The courage to accept an identity that is seen outside the social norm relies heavily on self-belief and self-esteem. It can be extremely challenging. For example, a trans person has a higher likelihood of suicide due to the social and political pressures of having this identity (Austin et al., 2022). Continuously seeing your identity as negative or feared has an impact on self-esteem. Self-esteem plays an important part in developing a sense of self, which in turn affects outcomes and achievements (Hamilton and Showunmi, 2023; Lane, 2008). Carrying the burden of being an outsider can be passed on through generations, based on social factors and can be worsened through acts that unleash a lifetime of grief and trauma (Adshead, 2024). In addition, when others do not acknowledge different identities then the disadvantages become harder to explain. In the example of the Black educator being stopped by the police, the disbelief of their experience leaves the individual to navigate confused feelings without acceptance of what was their reality. If prolonged, this has negative impacts on self-belief and self-esteem. hooks (2001: 93) discusses the concept of fear as the primary force upholding structures of domination. She writes, 'when we are taught that safety lies in sameness, then difference, of any kind, will appear as a threat'. Moving against fear, alienation and separation, choosing to connect and find similarities with others brings an articulation which counters the binary between systemic advantage and disadvantage. Froebelian perspectives align with hook's ideas of finding similarities and connections which will lead to finding a reflection of oneself in another.

Froebel explores identity through understanding an individual's fulfilment. He explains that this can only be found when there is self-recognition and knowledge of oneself. Recognizing difference and acknowledging the differing experiences and viewpoints is a step towards self-recognition (Liebschner, 1992). Individuals brave enough to be proud of their identity, particularly one that is viewed as outside the social norm, commit an act of resistance. By consciously addressing both the feeling of an insider and an outsider perspective can aid educators in more authentic work with children and families (Derman-Sparks et al., 2020).

When self-recognition is evident, it becomes possible to see the different 'intersections' crossed. The term 'intersectionality' was coined by Kimberle Crenshaw (2015). She described the term as a way to think about identity and its relationship to power. There are different social identities that hold different advantages or disadvantages. Each identity may give way to varying degrees of power within a society which we feel simultaneously. Having and knowing an identity, which intersects and develops an individual viewpoint and experience, is vital to understanding our relationships with ourselves, with others and then with the wider world.

The importance of educator self-awareness

One facet of being an educator is bringing personal experiences to practice, and continually forming an educator identity (Jawad, 2020). Becoming self-aware helps to reflect on practice and how self-perceptions can impact on professional relationships, with colleagues, children, families and external professionals. By being more open and aware there is more possibility to accept others, navigate tensions – including feedback, criticism and addressing any bias. Froebel's writing explains the need for all of those who work with children to be self-reflective. One way to explore this is to question why they are who they are today. This enables an individual to then be able to understand others (Froebel, 1826).

Hyland (2010) discusses the importance of cultural awareness and knowledge as another aspect to apply social justice in education. These aspects aid understanding of children and family backgrounds, heritages and ways of being. Awareness of how various cultures might experience the world helps us to understand children's experiences and identity. For example, Roshini's (aged three) childminder, Brenda, would offer her ham sandwiches. Roshini accepted these, unknowingly eating meat which her parents had requested her not to, due to cultural and religious beliefs. Brenda's lack of cultural knowledge and respect towards difference impacted Roshini's ability to express her own identity.

Diaz (2003) observed how language and bilingualism also play a part in identity and how children negotiate their identity in the contexts they are in. For example, Simi (aged four) spoke both English and Spanish. He told the educator that he is English and that he lives in London, but he is also from Ecuador. 'I have two places!' he explained. A culturally relevant educator needs to make a concerted effort to learn the cultural norms, experiences and values of the societal groups and communities with whom they work (Hyland, 2010). They need to use this knowledge to inform and adapt their practice as well as support children's articulation of their identity through careful listening and mindful interactions. Froebelian practice is used across the world and interwoven in cultural contexts in Aotearoa New Zealand, South Africa and Japan (Cooper and Rockel, 2024; Matsumura, 2024; Mbolekwa and Bruce, 2024). It is important that Froebelians understand that culture plays a huge role in early childhood education and they are able to make these links through children's learning.

Helping children to understand and realize their own identity

Educators have a moral imperative in supporting the development of children's identity as often children experience the impact of social injustice in their early childhood (Robinson and Diaz, 2016). In the United Nations Convention on the Rights of the Child (UNCRC) Article 8 and 29 highlight the right for children to preserve their identity and to develop it alongside their cultural identity, gender, religion and ethnic origins (UNICEF, 1989).

Children begin to attend education and early childhood settings during a formative part of their lives. They look to the educators and caregivers to help them work out who they are. Even very young children are developing concepts of similarities and differences whilst trying to make sense of these things. Studies have shown that even babies as young as six months' notice differences in skin colour and are drawn to those characteristics that are similar to their caregivers (Kelly et al., 2005). 'Stranger fear', a common behaviour that babies display when seeing someone with different characteristics to their caregivers, demonstrates how the brain makes connections and notices patterns with physical attributes (Louis and Betteridge, 2024).

Babies learn about themselves through their physical self. These include their eye movements tracking their caregivers and limb movements exploring the space around them. They develop interoception – a feeling of internal self needs and cry to communicate these needs. As mobility and movement develops, toddlers begin to work out how their feet and arms can move simultaneously. They see their environment from different perspectives. All this movement helps children to develop control of their body and increases confidence, impacting on self-esteem and a sense of self.

Children also notice how adults interact with their body, through transitions like nappy changing, soothing, feeding, moving together and learning who to trust. Their tone, gesture and touch interactions convey messages about themselves and their bodily autonomy (Bowlby, 1979; Goldschmied and Jackson, 2004; Manning-Morton, 2024; Winnicott, 1960). Much of Froebel's writing was based on observations of children with their families. He observed the child moving and beginning to understand themselves through their physical development. He included action songs and finger rhymes in Mother/Family songs (1844) specifically attuned to the movement of babies limbs, the rocking motion of lullabies and the bodily connections through heartbeat and brain development. Froebel's writing and observations of the impact of physical development is supported by contemporary research (Blythe, 2017; Goldschmied and Selleck, 1996; Manning-Morton, 2024; Powell and Goouch, 2019; The Froebel Trust, 2013).

Toddlers explore the world around them with the anchor of knowing a person they trust is close by (Manning-Morton, 2024; Winnicott, 1960). They can explore how things work, cause and effect, wearing familiar or unfamiliar clothing such as hats and shoes, possibly trying to work out where they begin and end, or trying out a different identity. Elijah (aged three) noticed Khadijah, his key person, wore a hijab so he used some material to cover his hair and they looked in the mirror together to see how they were similar. Children's internal self develops utilizing the feedback from the environment informing babies and young children of the feelings of safety, different emotions, moral understanding and values. Froebel knew that containment and attentiveness were intrinsic for many caregivers and he saw through his observations the way they responded to their child's cries and coos, this is further supported by Malloch and Trevarthen (2009); Trevarthen and Aitken's (2001) work on intersubjectivity and communicative musicality.

As children develop, they may demonstrate their identity through self-regulation and metacognition (McNair and Cerdan, 2022). These two concepts are closely linked as they are interdependent. Self-regulation may be observed when children try new things for themselves and may struggle and mutter to themselves. These 'mutterings' are described as private speech and are an indicator of self-regulation (Robson, 2010; Vygotsky, 1978; Whitebread et al., 2008). Children may also demonstrate metacognition; an awareness of their own or other's thinking. For example, Chris (aged five) was frustrated with another child who continued to pull his clothes whilst playing football. He explained to the educator that this child was not 'using their brain' and only thinking about pulling them instead of the rules of football. Children's ability to be metacognitive enables empathy with others. Being aware that one thinks demonstrates an awareness of consciousness, autonomy and agency. Froebel's educational principles were always to help children think, and he noticed as children grew older, they became more aware of how they were distinct from one another (Froebel, 1826; 1899).

Autonomy and identity are inextricably linked (Froebel Trust, 2021). Having agency and self-awareness ties in with being assertive (Manning-Morton, 2024). Being able to express your identity sometimes brings about an interesting and important subversion of what is intended. For example, during an 'I spy' game the educator wanted the children to guess 'boy' and pointed at Kameel (aged three), hinting 'What is Kameel?' He exclaimed 'I am a Black child!' demonstrating his sense of identity and bringing about a response which subverted the game. It is clear that Kameel has been told he is Black, and wears this identity proudly.

Identities around gender are important too. Gender differences are socialized in children. By the age of three children begin to group according to gender, with many educators having heard 'boys can't do that' in their settings (Xu, 2021). James and Rocco (aged three) were children who liked the film Frozen and wearing skirts. When they first met there was a realization of their shared interest. James said to Rocco 'Oh, you like girl's things too?' There was a sense of 'being seen' and acceptance from each other as though they finally had a friend who understood them. This visibility is vital and by drawing respectful attention to those who are less visible, hidden or even invisible is an act of social justice. Young children often learn about who is an 'insider' or 'outsider' according to societal norms and this impacts on their self-esteem and builds on biases and stereotypes if left unaddressed.

Significant adults in children's lives, including educators, have an important role in developing this sense of identity. A blind approach erases children's identity through ignoring differences. On the other hand, only focussing on narrow ideas of pain and struggle of those with a particular identity can create a single story experience instead of truly seeing the positives and accomplishments of that identity (Adichie, 2009; Yoon, 2023). The educator's role is important in dismantling unjustified norms and expectations and encouraging ways of creating more inclusive opportunity to express identity. When children are able to visualize a representation of their identity, they are able to see the possibilities of what they could be in the future. This may be in the form of stories and illustrations that challenge stereotypes providing children with alternative viewpoints or representing their own identity. The language used can play a part in perpetuating as well as dismantling identity. For example, making assumptions unnecessarily categorizes children when gendered language is used such as 'Such a strong boy!'. These comments and phrases assign stereotypes to children which can be assimilated into children's thinking if continuously heard and confirmed. Being aware of what is said to children is important. It has an impact on one's thinking as well as a child's internal thinking. Using language that is inclusive, clear and accurate allows children to make up their own minds about who they are.

Throughout the chapter, the exploration of identity and interlinking with Froebelian practice has been evident in aligning the different concepts together. He wrote how knowing oneself never reaches a fixed point, instead develops in accordance with others and the world around, placing this work within a decolonial lens. He knew the importance of self-awareness, which can only be found when reflecting on oneself (Bruce, 2021; Pascal et al., 2026).

> 'Froebel's basic educational aim, that of life-unity, can ultimately only come about by self-knowledge. Self-knowledge however is only made possible by standing outside oneself and comparing the self as it is, with the self as it ought to be. The self as it is, can only be judged by the actions which that self has performed so far. One's actions were therefore the mediator between one's true self and the self one aspired to be.' (Liebschner, 1992: 137)

With this critical consciousness, educators are able to fulfil their pedagogical responsibility in supporting the holistic development of children's identity.

CHAPTER 3

Diversity

This chapter focuses on how the individual relates to others amidst their developing identity and interpersonal relationships. Exploring identity is a step towards social justice, but looking at self-identity without looking at how one relates to others creates isolation. This breeds a feeling of competition or fear particularly when there is a lack of understanding and a hierarchical viewpoint of one another (Brodie, 2007; Grimaldi, 2011; hooks, 2001). A world-view that aligns with a collectivist culture, like Māori people, looks to celebrate and express identity whilst also being a member of a community (Cooper, 2025).

> But as we act, we not only express what is in us and help give shape to the world; we also receive what is outside us and reshape our inner selves. (hooks, 2001: 77)

A setting celebrated a 'Heritage Day' where children and staff wore traditional clothes. Within one room there were many different heritages including Belinda an Eritrean girl wearing a Habesha Kemis, Kos wearing Polish and Portuguese flag colours and Santi wearing an Ecuador football shirt. They represented a multitude of heritages with children of similar ages, who all lived locally and attended the setting. Together they were a group but individually they all had distinct identities. They could be described as being diverse. The term *diversity* is heard in many places. In education, diversity might relate to the variety of characteristics of the children, families or staff teams. These characteristics might include racial, ethnic, socioeconomic, geographic and professional differences (Diverse Educators, 2024). In its simplest form, diversity means difference.

Diversity explores the ways in which the individual maintains their uniqueness whilst simultaneously belonging to a group where there are similarities, and developing relationships with each other. It is important to start by focusing on the whole and finding what commonalities there are. Working in this way creates a sense of belonging – feeling like an insider (Gregory and Ruby, 2011). This enables an exploration of the differences. Froebel in his writings may not have explicitly discussed diversity in the way the term is used today, but in his actions and implicitly embedded in his pedagogy and principles we can see the celebration of individuality and connection with others as being of utmost importance in his ideas about children and education. The Froebelian principles of 'Relationships Matter' and 'Unity and Connectedness' form the basis of diversity (Froebel Trust, 2021). Whinnett (2024) emphasizes a strengths-based approach which recognizes and values the expertise from others and informs how to enable a sense of belonging for each child and their family.

Three pictorial representations are used to interpret Froebel's concept of interconnection alongside Bronfenbrenner's (1986) ecological systems model and Furman's (2012) dimensions of social justice (see Figures 3.1, 3.2 and 3.3). Each image uses concentric circles to demonstrate the individual and the relationship with others. The images are circular. They do not move in a linear fashion. There is an entanglement of time, space and effect. They weave, ebb, flow and plateau throughout these dimensions and relationships.

Froebel emphasized the role of the individual in their purpose to contribute to the community, including an element of reciprocity within the relationship. This chapter explores the concept of 'Who am I in relation to others, and how do others aid in my understanding of self?'

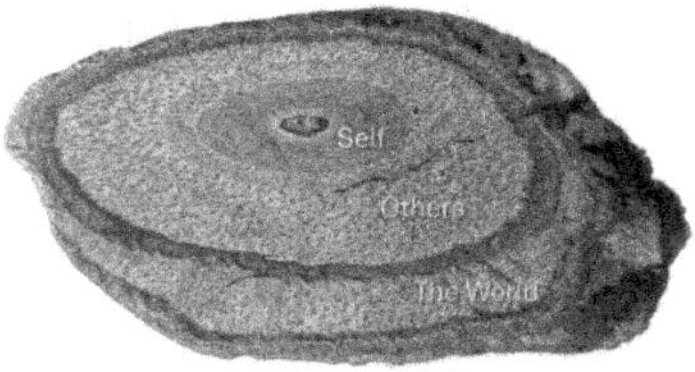

FIGURE 3.1 Froebelian framework of self, others and the world adapted from Joshi (2023).

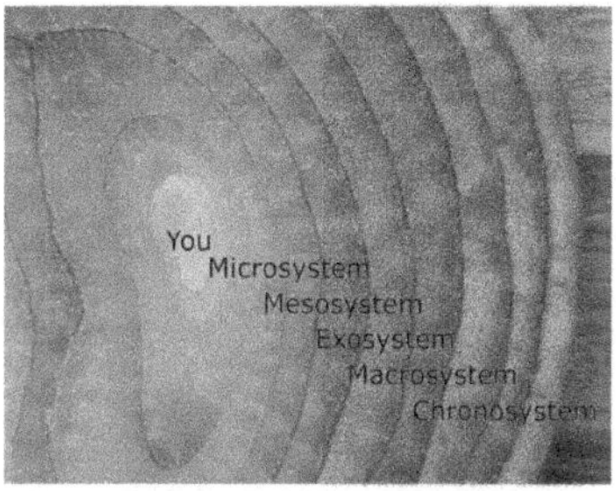

FIGURE 3.2 Ecological systems model adapted from Bronfenbrenner (1986). Represented through a cross section of an onion. Each layer standing for each system.

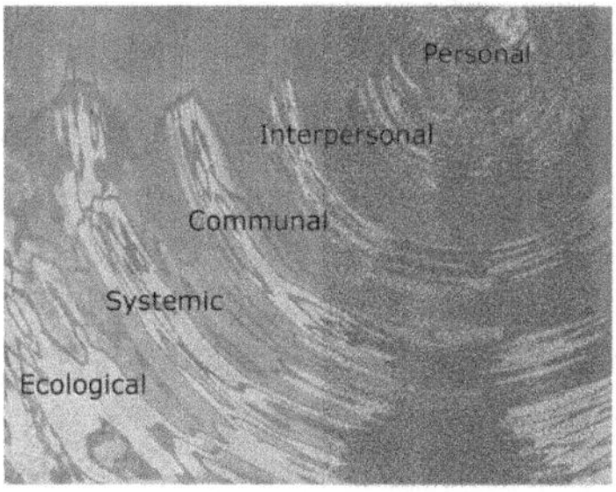

FIGURE 3.3 Dimensions of social justice adapted from Furman (2012).

Hierarchies of difference

Intersectionality (discussed in Chapter 2) and the hierarchies of difference are interlinked. The hierarchies of difference can be described by the existence of comfort and entitlement with certain types of equity and varying discomfort with others (Konayashi and Ray, 2000; Robinson and Diaz, 2016). For example, in the UK, those from the Gypsy, Roma and Traveller community are often marginalized through penalizing their nomadic nature (Crew, 2024; James, 2021). These hierarchies are maintained in society and visible in the microcosm of settings and schools. Many educators unknowingly perpetuate and normalize these hierarchies through practice, pedagogy, curriculum and interactions. In many settings there is an upholding of heteronormative views which is automatically accepted as conventional. This hierarchy ignores of the interconnection and intersectionality between all characteristics. Questioning and reflecting on these hierarchies of difference supports educators in working to remove it altogether.

Children may be subconsciously attuned to these hierarchies of difference. This can influence their behaviour towards themselves and others (Katz and Kofkin, 1997). Those who belong to less socially acceptable hierarchies may be experiencing confusing and difficult emotions about their place in the world, lacking a sense of belonging, not feeling valued. For example, when Harmony was playing in the role play, she rejected the Black doll as she was told by another child that her skin, and the dolls skin 'looked like poo'. This interaction is unfortunately not an uncommon experience for many Black and Brown children. It hugely impacts self-esteem and a child's feeling of self-worth. Many children will have different ideas and opinions, many of which are formed by things they might see and hear. Educators have a pedagogical responsibility of acting upon issues and nurturing children's identity. Responding to these situations carefully and sensitively, ensures that children understand what they have said is not acceptable and why. Educators need to hold space for the child who has been a victim of this situation and ensure that they feel psychologically safe and empowered by who they are (Louis and Betteridge, 2024). Socially just practice considers how educators are ensuring a free expression of identity as well as supporting them in belonging to the setting. Leaders need to ensure their teams are trained in how to respond to these situations effectively, this in turn supports the erasure of the hierarchies of difference.

By being curious and reflecting on observations of children's interactions and play, educators can ensure assumptions are unpicked by developing empathy and providing a wider perspective that enables all children to belong. Clark and Clark (1996) used a Black and white doll to explore children's feelings about race. This study showed how all children, whatever race they were, noticed these hierarchies of difference by choosing the white doll as 'beautiful' and 'good' and the Black doll as 'ugly' and 'naughty'. The study, called the Black Doll Test, is played out in many settings across the world. Educators need to address this by ensuring that all dolls are cared for equally, and when children make choices about which doll to use, they draw out their reasoning and continue to offer children alternative viewpoints that are framed within a socially just perspective. Froebel wrote 'every child should be accepted as an indispensable and essential member of the human race', in this he is describing the individuality and diversity of children and their sense of belonging to the human race (Lilley, 1967: 57). He also describes the role of the family and educator in nurturing these differences in children, accepting them as whoever they are.

Professional hierarchies

Within early childhood education and care there are multiple agencies and professionals that interconnect with one another supporting the child at different stages of their life. It is important that there is a holistic shared approach that supports the whole family. An early education conference organized by a local council purposely invited a range of professionals to present and attend the conference. This included health practitioners, nurses, midwives, educational psychologists, speech and language therapists and family support workers alongside educators and leaders in education. This provided a space for connection and developed a joined-up approach for all those who impact the lives of children ensuring holistic support for the family. By removing the silos of professional hierarchy and conflicting agendas, it held the family at the centre, and ensured that children were kept at the heart of the work (Brent Council, 2024). This multi-agency way of working aligns closely to Froebelian ideas, he advocated for removing the separation of subjects, and finding coherence and unity. He specifically writes, 'never forget the function of a school is not to teach and communicate many things but to bring out the unity which inheres in all' (Lilley, 1967: 139).

Recognition theory

Honneth's (2014) theory of recognition can be taken through a decolonial lens, which looks to remove the social categorization put upon individuals to conform to dominant societies. He builds upon these ideas by focusing on the relationship between individuation and socialization. By taking the simple act of recognizing someone, there is an admittance that they are an autonomous being. Wholly recognizing someone who has a certain feature or characteristic, their features are embraced and autonomy recognized. This impacts psychologically and instils a sense of belonging. For example, when a baby babbles towards a parent and they have this interaction returned, it provides an affirmation of existence and enables the development of identity. These ideas add onto Trevarthen's

(2001) work on intersubjectivity between caregivers and babies. Through this we see how vital it is to have positive interactions with those close to us as these enable our identity and sense of self.

Beljan (2025) explores this concept further by drawing attention to the space in between these interactions. The concept of resonance is the interaction and the preceding connection and reaction. For example, when a parent interacts with their baby, this may be returned with a smile. The interaction suggests a resonance, instead of repulsion or indifference. The resonance is then expressed through the smile. There is a transformation of these internal and external feelings and sense of self. Froebel's understanding of the inner and the outer and the connection between can be used to explain this expressivity. This double articulation stems from Humbolts and Hegel's work around Romanticism which along with early concepts of recognition theory was being researched and philosophized during Froebel's time (Jena, 2020; Wulf, 2023). What is unique about Froebel's work is how he articulated these influences into his ideas for education (Brians, 2017).

The United Nations Convention on the Rights of the Child (UNCRC) embodies recognition theory in its language and approach. It also builds on Freirean concepts of critical consciousness which rely on understanding the interconnection of relationships and recognizing the space and positionality that one takes. This highlights the role of an individual in enabling the development of another. Underpinning the UNCRC is the notion that to be recognized, we must depend on others, and therefore we are dependent on the cooperation with others (Thomas and Stoecklin, 2018).

Recognition theory highlights the need to recognize or the struggle to recognize all individuals, characteristics, groups and communities. For example, when educators take on a 'colour blind' approach this is a message to children that they do not recognize the different skin colours that children have and therefore the different attitudes, intersections and hierarchies that come with this. Recognition of communities and countries can be taken to a political lens, for example, in 2024, nine countries formally recognized Palestine. By doing so, they politically recognized the struggle of the Palestinian people and supported the humanization of these people (Al Jazeera, 2024; Iser, 2019).

Misrecognition of one another builds a 'fear of the other'. This can be seen in young children when they demonstrate 'Stranger fear' (Sroufe, 1977). This is where babies who see someone who does not resemble their immediate parent or caregiver become distressed and upset. As they grow older, they become more comfortable with others who may not look like their parents as they begin to recognize and be exposed to different features, abilities, skin colours, hair types and so on. Whilst this example of 'stranger fear' highlights the physical differences, there are social, political and ideological views that individuals have, and we must reflect on whether these are recognized in educational spaces. When individuals meet those who are unfamiliar it can naturally bring a sense of discomfort. However, utilizing recognition theory and Froebelian ideas ensures that educators recognize, value and wholly accept each child and family. Janet, a new parent, had a strong viewpoint on breastfeeding, advocating that this was the best for babies and nothing else was good enough. Daisy, another parent, had many challenges with breastfeeding and therefore decided to use formula and bottles. When Janet heard that Daisy was using formula, she criticized her decision. Janet refused to recognize Daisy's situation and therefore dehumanized her and her choices, and instilled a hierarchy of what was acceptable and what was not. This example demonstrates how experiences cannot be generalized and what works for some may not work for others. By recognizing that each individual navigates life and overcome obstacles in different ways widens the possibilities of multiple solutions instead of narrowing into binary concepts of right and wrong.

Developing a sense of belonging

There are multiple ways to ensure that children and families feel that they belong as part of a community and their beliefs and values are recognized. The role of the educator is to ensure that they fully understand and recognize the needs of these families and represent them within the setting, this places a huge importance on nurturing relationships. It also draws attention to the hierarchies of difference.

Annual Christmas celebrations and performances that include re-enacting the birth of Jesus are often an exciting time of the year for many children, families and educators. However the production of the nativity can exclude those who don't celebrate Christmas and places importance on a Christian celebration demonstrating a hierarchy of religion (Joshi, 2023a). Hannah's Jehovah's Witness faith meant she could not be involved in the nativity. The educators adapted what they usually did during this time to be more inclusive by coming together to sing familiar nursery rhymes with adapted lyrics to include winter themes. Hannah and her family were happy to join in and therefore felt included as part of the end-of-year celebrations. If a Muslim family shared that they would not be able to join in with celebrations, the question arises, how this would be received, and whether they would have a similar reaction to that in the situation of Hannah's family. In the UK, analysis of parliamentary and media debates demonstrates an increase in xenophobic and Islamophobic language (Montiel-McCann and Julios-Costa, 2025). This means educators must be active in developing a sense of belonging through a social justice lens.

For Froebel, culture, religion and spirituality are embedded throughout his work. His ideas around these topics present as panentheism (Bruce, 2021; Neumann, 2024). This is an understanding of God's existence in all things (Sachs, 2003). Froebel's work offers the existence of an invisible third within the field of children's education. This could be interpreted as the sense of belonging to a culture, religion or spirituality towards life and humanity.

Language is continually evolving and can support or diminish recognition of difference. For example, the British values that are encompassed within British educational frameworks uses the word 'tolerate' (Department for Education, 2014). This can be read to imply that care, nurture or respect is not needed. The organization Diverse Educators (2025) instead offers the phrase 'be where you are celebrated not tolerated'. In this, their approach is to embrace all differences and recognize individuals equally and uphold a reciprocal relationship.

Farah (2024) discusses the lack of recognition that occurs in many models of language and linguistic support. She explains the roots of assessment in this area come from standardization which disregards difference and diversity within language (Nair, Farah and Cushing, 2023). Farah's view is that there is no wrong way to speak and that educators must have an emancipatory practice that creates spaces and places of nurturing diversity of language.

This aligns closely with Froebel's ideas as he writes 'Language, which gives expression to the constant movement of the life of the mind, must reveal the qualities and characteristics of life. It must be flexible to the highest degree if man is to reveal his whole being in all its aspects' (Lilley, 1967: 152). Froebel valued the expression of the child in whichever form suited the child, he knew that language is an important form of communication that expresses children's inner worlds to the outer and showing the outer their diversity.

Recognition of children's neurodivergence, differing abilities or medical conditions is often drawn from a deficit approach (Murphy, 2022). This lacks the recognition of each individual's identity and capability. Zoe explained how her daughter, Melissa (aged five), had a rare condition which caused fear and apprehension from the educators as they were concerned how they would support Melissa's needs. The educator's mistake was to only focus on her physical needs and care, which whilst important, did not see Melissa's interests, personality or capability. The fear of the educators came from a place of not knowing and being unable to see Melissa as a whole. The leaders within the setting arranged a meeting with the family to ensure that any worries were dispelled and in collaboration they developed an approach that would help Melissa thrive in their setting whilst also maintaining her health. Using a Froebelian perspective enables educators to look at what they can do in the situation they are in, and building on the foundational principles to guide through what might be a new circumstance. This is familiar to many educators who navigated through the COVID-19 pandemic by finding new ways to work whilst still maintaining children's education (Green, 2024).

The role of diversity within social justice is about ensuring individual identities are protected, recognized and have a sense of belonging to the community they are part of. Social justice celebrates difference and community, as does Froebel when he writes about 'individuality, diversity and unity' (Froebel, 1826: 20). He reminds us that there are no homogenous groups and each individual will encounter and navigate situations differently. Celebrating diversity enables educators to recognize and understand the different experiences children will have. This relies on a strong relationship and cultural knowledge of each individual family. Shifting positionality of educator to learner can empower children and families in sharing a part of themselves to be celebrated. When enough time is spent on cultivating and nurturing relationships, the process of social justice becomes more embedded and impactful.

CHAPTER 4

Equality

This chapter explores the social justice theme of equality, examining what this looks like in practice, and how or whether it exists within settings and communities. This requires interrogation of the socio-cultural and political frameworks intended to uphold equality in many societies today. Equality is defined by the concept of fairness, and together with opportunity, this offers a starting point. When there is a sense of fairness it establishes a feeling of safety and choice.

Froebel's writings embody an ideology for a type of institution and collective communal living that was available and accessible for all. Froebel's personal challenges with relationships, particularly with his father, meant he strived for nurturing families and communities with a reciprocal relationship between the child and others (Lilley, 1967).

Abundance of resources

A group of children were filling and pouring cylinders using spoons in the water area. There were not enough spoons or cylinders for each child to have their own, so Robin (aged two) took a cylinder from Bolu (aged two) which disrupted Bolu's exploration. Bolu reacted by shouting and stamping his feet. Across the room, Sharon, reacting to the outcry, called out 'No more water for you Bolu!' Another educator, Yara, who had observed this interaction, instead found more cylinders and spoons for the children to use so that they could all join in with the experience of filling and emptying.

It is challenging in settings to be able to observe every interaction that occurs between children. It demonstrates the common occurrence of biases and immediate reactions to solve problems and maintain calm. When biases are relied on too often, scapegoating can occur. Scapegoating is when an individual is unfairly blamed and shamed for the mistakes of others. Mistakes are a vital part of learning; they enable a reflection of moral understanding and empathy. The learning environment in all aspects – physical, emotional, cognitive and spiritual needs to support children's ability to reflect on mistakes, problem solve and test out notions of kindness and fairness. Educators who aspire to be patient and nurturing work to avoid their biases. Those with a tendency to accept mistakes more from some children than others bring about the hierarchies of difference discussed in the previous chapter (Drew et al., 2023). The educator who understands the context of the interactions and has meaningful relationships with the children is best placed to support children in their self-reflection.

In the observation, Yara reflects the seemingly simple solution of ensuring that children have access to enough resources. Children require sufficient resources to alleviate the need for turn taking which can be too demanding for younger ages. This enables children to be able to carry out their investigations and develop confidence and skill with the resources they are using. Joshi (2023b) discusses the intrinsic need for children to be able to bring resources from place to place and ensuring that there is an abundance of resources for children to use. These do not need to be expensive items, instead collectable, natural and recyclable materials are just as interesting to children. This is pertinent as in contexts such as informal settlements in South Africa scarcity of resources mean that an abundance of certain items may be difficult to obtain. In one setting, recycled and everyday materials were used to create musical instruments ensuring all children were able to take part in making music (see Figures 4.1 and 4.2).

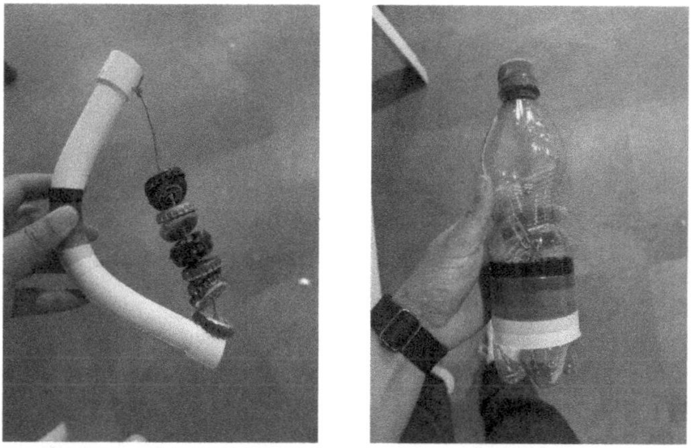

FIGURES 4.1 and 4.2 Instruments made from recycled materials.

Bruce (2023) discusses how children's play agenda will have a drive to create something which may include bringing in items from all over the setting. Ensuring that children know where they can take from to enable their creation instead of taking from another child who is engaged in their own play agenda is an important rule to establish to maintain equality, fairness and access to resources. Even very young children soon learn not to transfer paints, or blocks from wooden block sets, whilst knowing it is alright to transfer recycled material from the workshop area to use in the water tray. Educators need to support children's understanding of the environment and how it is structured. This helps children to learn and feel confident about the materials and resources they find interesting to use. It also helps them to feel safe and valued in the community they spend time in. Froebel's vision for kindergarten ensured resources were open-ended and plentiful. The Gifts that he designed demonstrate this open-endedness which were later developed into the unit blocks that are seen in many settings today (Whinnett, 2020). Froebel wrote about how he spent much of his childhood outdoors, with the privilege of an abundance of nature. Here, he found that nature was an all-encompassing and remarkable tool for education. He was able to explore the tiny detailed creatures to the expansive rolling hills and forests. This is later reflected in his kindergarten where children had individual gardens and access to a shared communal garden (Froebel, 1861). The communal garden stood as a model which enabled children to understand how to care for their own gardens.

Family unity and holistic development

Shyla and Vanessa, two parents of children with additional learning needs, developed a friendship. Shyla supported Vanessa in advocating for her son, suggesting he play in the park, offered to help with school collection and encouraged her to attend meetings with the educators when discussing his development and learning.

Families who know how to advocate and access the resources available to them can share information with others. This can bring about empowerment, a feeling of autonomy and participation (Yoon, 2023). Belonging to a community, relationships with families and between families is vital for all but particularly for those families who have children with additional needs as this experience can be incredibly lonely (Kalalo, 2024). Froebel said, 'several families would unite themselves in this associated nurture of life and bring together their children as if to a genuine family festival' (Froebel, 1861: 162). In Froebel's vision for education an importance was placed on the family and a collection of families coming together. All with the idea of educating their children at an institution that develops children's individuality, diversity and unity.

Hall (2025) describes the system of schools and institutions as a space that shapes the inequalities that exist. Whilst educational settings have the inference of equality, not all children and families experience early childhood education in the same way. Overcoming the barriers by establishing processes which: share information freely, enable access to information and maintain clear explanations are all starting points for equality to exist in the educational space. This can be done through friendships within the community, but also through the systems that prioritize and cater for these relationships. Connecting the home and setting together centres around family participation. Athey (1990) writes how educators can 'illuminate practice' which invites families to discuss their child's learning. Remembering that not all families have equitable access, so utilizing organizations like 'Storybook Dads' who create audio recordings of stories read by parents who are in prison, can support participation (Brookes and Frankham, 2021; Morgan et al., 2013). This ensures that all families are able to access and participate in their child's learning which can improve children's outcomes (Pungello et al., 2009). Froebelian ways of working with families are integrating, providing access and fostering belonging. This can include creating toy libraries, home packs, cooking bags and trips to the local library to help access the services there (Gura, 1996). Further examples include: parent invitations to stay and play sessions, letters provided in different languages and providing a variety of ways to access the same information such as online, in letters, website links and with pictures to support the text and face to face discussions.

Froebel's work and writing prioritized educating the whole child. In his final work, the Family (Mother) songs, he provided different forms of development (Froebel, 1844). This included: physical development through hand and finger movements, emotional development through bond and attachment, moral development and linking to everyday life through the meaningful words chosen for the songs, and an introduction into symbolism and representation through hand gestures and detailed illustrations that could represent something from everyday life. Through this holistic and multi modal way of educating, he ensured that all children and families could be involved and access each part or whole that was significant for them.

Adult and child worlds

Communities need to behave collectively to enable equality and bring about the systemic adaptions required. The insider/outsider perspectives from Chapter 2 can be applied to the context of adult/child worlds with the adult being the insider and the child the outsider (Gregory and Ruby, 2011; Robinson and Diaz, 2016). Critical thinking towards the different child and adult worlds can strengthen the views of children as active citizens of society. McCormack et al. (2024: 330) explore participation methodologies with children and families with the intention to 'support a more democratic culture'. Currently, the world of the adult and the world of the child are disconnected even though these worlds collide continually through what is offered or not offered. For example, in many cities there are play spaces for children. These spaces are fenced and gated determining where children can be. Signs with 'No ball games' can be found in residential spaces limiting children's play choices. Whilst there is an offering to children these spaces are provided through an adult gaze. Excluding children from taking part in the process of creating these places distances the adult and child worlds further. The creation of play spaces appropriate for children is left to children who transform mundane adult worlds into children's worlds using imagination and play as an empowering tool (Gemayel, 2024). For Froebel, the idea of segregated spaces for children were not in his vision. He believed that children should be integral to the community. His quote 'come let us live with our children' (Froebel, 1861: 3) explains how children should be a member of the whole and play a part in learning from and giving to the community (Schamberger, 2024).

Froebel wrote about what he observed through children's play which he saw children expressing a higher form of their consciousness. Play offered a deepening of imagination and creativity. In the heterotopias that Gemayel (2024) imagines, children find ways to play when the conditions are right for them even if the environment is limited. Tying together Froebelian and Freirean perspectives, democratic and participatory practices which interweave adult and child worlds enables an education for freedom and critical thinking (McCormack et al., 2024).

Relevant accurate curricula

Enabling equality within educational settings raises questions, critiques and assessment of the current policies and systems in place for children and their families. Curriculum programmes and the learning environment invites an opportunity to reflect on questions such as: what is included in curricula, why these choices are made and who is creating these programmes.

Staff in a setting dutifully celebrated Diwali showing children henna patterns drawn on hands. Unknown to the educators, henna is used as a celebration across many cultures and religions and not just for Diwali, which is the Hindu festival of lights. An incomplete representation of this celebration was shared with the children. This example demonstrates the missed opportunities for critical reflection. It highlights the need for educators to deepen their cultural knowledge, ability to research and find authentic representation grounded in accurate respectful and representative curricula (Hyland, 2010).

Leaders in one setting carefully planned a responsive professional development programme. This included time to reflect on the cohort of children, and space to consider the different identities and diversities of the children. They considered how they could incorporate and reflect this in their environment and curriculum. The educators met with families to develop the curriculum together empowering both educators in their understanding of the community, as well as families in having a say and participating in their child's learning. The high importance that Froebel placed on his ideas for education meant that the educators needed to be trained specifically for the education and care of childhood. He knew the importance of supporting families in their role as first educators, so working closely with families helps to ensure parents understand how to continue their child's education at home (Lilley, 1967).

Educator networks and collaboration

Developing the collaborative approach can extend within local networks. For example, staff in a group of neighbouring settings worked together to improve their community links, responding to what was needed. This included a shared approach to flexible timings between settings, food bank access and opportunities to garden and grow plants with the children and families. The network also utilized training opportunities for the educators by pooling together resources and purchasing group training and arranging peer meetings. Working in this way, the staff felt empowered, supported by their peers and developed their knowledge and interests for their practice. Educators need to participate in their profession as being a knowledgeable educator requires commitment to a lifelong journey of learning.

Sometimes, when there is a disagreement of pedagogical approaches, tensions can arise. This can come in the form of 'professional disobedience', which Selina enacted by creating an environment in a particular way when being observed, and then reverting back afterwards (Archer, 2021). Joining early childhood educational organizations gave her the confidence and theoretical backing to successfully take on a leadership role to enact her ideas for pedagogy and practice in the setting.

Froebel knew the impact of well-trained educators on the education he envisioned. By creating an institution for teacher training he empowered individuals in having a role within the community. This in turn had a huge impact on the many women who undertook his training and spread his pedagogy across Germany and further afield such as UK, United States and Japan (Read, 2019).

Global and local level organizations such as the World Organisation for Early Childhood Education (OMEP), Early Education and the National Association for the Education of Young Children (NAEYC) are examples of policy driven and principle led organizations which advocate for children's education within their remits. Educators who become members belong to a collective who believe in the organization's causes. OMEP demonstrates their clear goals which include committing to 'educating for peace and human rights' (OMEP, 2025). For educators, finding these places provides a sense of direction and a wider network to voice needs at local level and find pathways for change and equality.

Educator burnout and its impact on retention within the field is rising high across the globe (McDaniel et al., 2024). Being able to rest, have space for professional dialogue and a focus on well-being are ways in which burnout and illness can be reduced (Cave in Goddard, 2024). The Reflection with Guidance tool used by leaders to facilitate discussions and encourage active participation, strengthened educator's professional development, knowledge and fostered a sense of empowerment (Pascal et al., 2026). Froebelian education not only looks at the pedagogical approach to teaching and learning, but also guides leadership. By embodying the Froebelian approach, leaders can reflect on their methods of supporting their team and how they do so in a way which aligns with their principles and values.

Frameworks of equality

The framework of social justice that is used throughout this book builds upon the individual and connects to others. The Universal Declaration of Human Rights (UDHR) is an aspect of social justice situating itself within broader socio-political, economic and environmental contexts. Remaining critical of the frameworks that are used, ensures transparency and awareness of possible Western ideology and colonial gaze.

Adopting a decolonial lens, Veer and Dezentje (2023) explore the cultural perspectives of human rights, explaining that often there are religious, customary, social and cultural norms which also uphold fundamental human rights. They discuss how in Global Majority societies such as African and Asian countries, the focus is on collective communities. For example, Confucianism in China is concerned with communal duties. In African countries, the Ubuntu philosophy 'I am because we are' upholds the notion of humanity and connections with others. The Manden Charter based in West Africa is considered one of the oldest constitutions in the world, beginning in the thirteenth century and held through oral form, it advocates social peace in diversity, education, integrity of the motherland, food security and freedom of expression among many others principles (UNESCO, 2008). In India, there are women-led courts called Nari Adalats that function outside state-led mechanisms. These initiatives and systems are more likely to be sustainable as they build on community and collective needs (Kethineni et al., 2016).

When formulating the UDHR, wider cultural perspectives and philosophies were not included and therefore the western ideals of human rights prevailed. In the documentation, there is little mention of community, collective and connective importance. Instead, the UDHR focuses mostly on the individual's rights. Although, Article 29 mentions the duty of the individual to the community this relates back to the development of the individual (United Nations, 1948). Human Rights are not a sole act or responsibility. Interpersonal and communal connections are vital in having a full life.

The United Nations Convention of the Rights of the Child (UNCRC) *First Call for Children* (1989) was built upon the UDHR in later years. It's creation demonstrated the change in thinking towards children and their space, value and rights in society (UNICEF, 2025). It was particularly prevalent following industrialization where it was common to have children working alongside adults in unsanitary and unsafe conditions. There was a growing consensus of the injustices of these practices, alongside a larger movement focussing on the understanding and developmental needs of children moving towards a policy to protect children. Froebel's context for his ideas come from the time period following the Napoleonic war. In his letters, he writes about his thinking around society, community and individuals. These ideas are threaded through his writing and underpinned through notions of unity and connectedness (Liebschner, 1992). These concepts bring about a dialogue of what is appropriate for children based upon the adult/child worlds.

In Scotland the UNCRC has become part of the law as of 2024 setting a precedent to embed children's rights into all aspects of society (Scottish Government, 2024). On the other hand, the United States of America is the only UN state which has not ratified the UNCRC. One reason given by some objectors is that the policies are already in place, whilst others state it infringes on parental rights, participatory rights and juvenile justice laws (Lichtsinn and Goldhagen, 2023). A critical review of the UNCRC embodiment of equality and whether children were involved in developing these rights addresses the possible underlying Romanticism of the innocence of children or an awareness of 'saviourism' when considering how to protect children, and what they should be protected from. Across the globe, there are many examples of political motivations claiming to protect children which in reality, compromise or harm their rights. These motivations are strategically threaded through rhetoric such as anti-transgender legislation, banning books and using health myths to undermine vaccinations of children.

Whilst the UNCRC have advanced children's rights through permeating education and political movements, gaps remain in meeting these ideals. In 2015 United Nations Member States adopted the 2030 agenda for sustainable development through which the seventeen Sustainable Development Goals (SDGs) provide holistic frameworks for global partnership and action (United Nations, 2015). It remains important to focus on the interconnection of all goals through the pillars of sustainability – social, environmental and economic, pictorially represented in Figure 4.3.

However, the emphasis on economic growth in many countries and societies tips this balance and creates an unsustainable model (Boussemart et al., 2020). Bhutan offers an alternative viewpoint with its measure of Gross National Happiness (GNH). These outcomes connect human rights and cultural-spiritual roots into a society that promotes well-being (Norren, 2023). It embodies collective community approaches and promotes South African Ubuntu principles and a Māori worldview that individuals advance when others advance too (Cooper, 2025; Ngubane and Makua, 2021b). Each of these frameworks (UDHR, UNCRC, SDGs) asks countries, governments and organizations to work towards equality, through removing structural barriers in place that impede on fairness and access to opportunities.

Achieving equality requires a sense of belonging, community and liberation for those who are outsiders, marginalized or oppressed. Equality emphasizes the need to be imaginative and to seek alternative methods to enable fairness and opportunity. During his time Froebelian education was seen as radical or difficult to achieve, but in his letters he writes 'Everyone wants a way of education such as I have described here, but no one

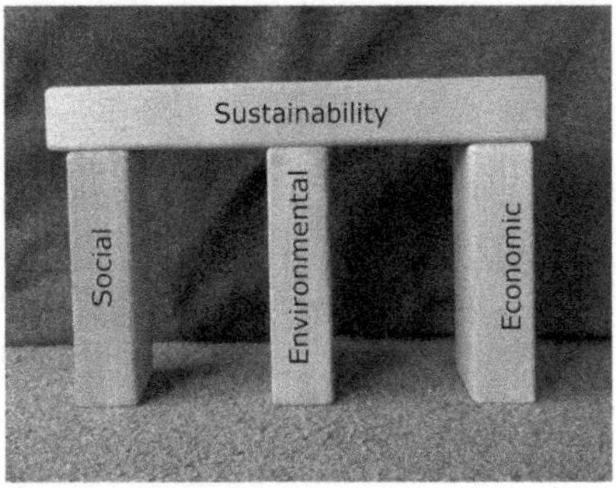

FIGURE 4.3 The three pillars of sustainability.

is willing to seize the obvious means to achieve it' (Lilley, 1967: 172). He implies that corrupt and bureaucratic systems refuse to take a step in any direction and refuse to financially fund and support a new way of thinking. The systems in place in today's society require listening, reflection and collaboration with participants in order to make changes that support social justice. Whilst infrastructures are not necessarily changed overnight, a Froebelian philosophy and collective action with critical consciousness provides a hopeful pathway to imagining a better world. A strategic approach that systematically removes barriers and addresses the establishment and institutions that uphold inequitable practices is what is most needed (Chamberlin, 1970).

CHAPTER 5

Equity

The concept of equity is grounded in the reality that not all starting points are the same, and working in an equitable way can provide the means towards equality. Together they are key principles in the possibility of achieving social justice.

Within this sphere of social justice, there is always the question of who is holding the power. Who is 'giving' equity to others, and who is taking it away? (Bateson and Tembo, 2024). Guiding these discussions on social justice is the recognition of oppression and domination with society. Welcoming difference dismantles the structures, processes, concepts and categories that uphold indifferent policies. A social restructure is required which builds on contributions from all groups (Eisenberg, 2006). Furman (2012) uses the dimensions of social justice to help articulate these ideas at different levels (see Figure 5.1). Within each circle there are ways of working which support equitable and democratic approaches.

Educators can embody equity through recognizing who and where the child is at in their development and learning, and building on what they already know. Froebelian educators understand that children are all unique and so is their development. Therefore their starting points differ based on their experiences of the world (Tovey, 2017, 2020). This Froebelian idea is supported by Moll et al. (1992) who discuss the 'funds of knowledge' describing the bank from which children draw their knowledge from. These can

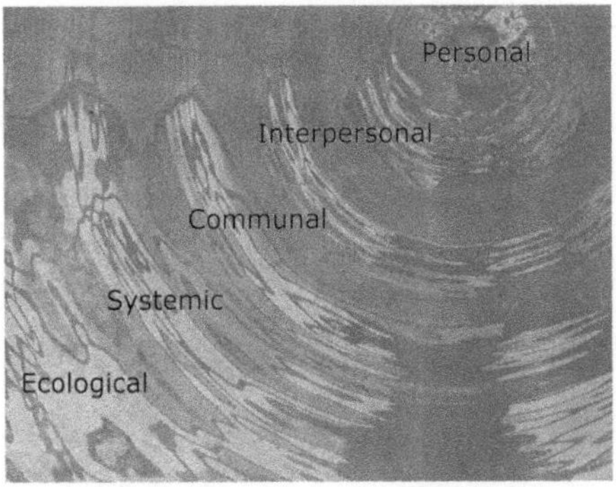

FIGURE 5.1 Dimensions of social justice adapted from Furman (2012).

exacerbate the insider/ outsider perspective that children, families and educators might hold. Recognizing this enables educators to ensure that these barriers are removed to develop a sense of belonging. The freedoms, introduced in this chapter, offer a guide to remove learning obstacles and consider perspectives and circumstances that exist for individuals and families.

Equitable practice within the setting

Institutions like early childhood educational settings can often have rules that are blindly enforced. For example, the letter in the Figure 5.2 is the response that Rakesh received when he informed the setting that his daughter, Radhi (aged four) would not be attending school on Monday due to a religious celebration. Rakesh expressed his disappointment in the setting's inability to empathize and recognize the family's religious beliefs and celebrations.

The setting could have seen how this was an important opportunity for Radhi to celebrate with her family and learn

[redacted] [redacted]

[redacted] [redacted]

Our Ref: [redacted] 8th November, 1996

Dear [redacted],

Mrs. [redacted] informs me that [redacted] will be absent from school on Monday. Generally, it is a matter of common courtesy to request permission for a child to be absent from school, other than for illness, after which an explanatory note is required.

The visit to the New Walk Museum has been organized for many weeks and was on the list of advance dates you received at the beginning of term. The visit is linked with the work the children have been doing, and will do, following the visit.

I hope that you will change your view and that [redacted] will be able to attend on Monday.

Yours sincerely,

[redacted]

Headmaster

FIGURE 5.2 Letter to Rakesh.

about her religion and culture. The setting enforced its power through the language used within the letter, suggesting that the institution should be held at high importance, and required permission to be absent from it. Equitable practices would have encouraged the leaders to understand the importance for children to celebrate their religion, and enable a positive sense of religious identity (Lane, 2008). By thinking ahead, the setting could have better planned the trip, and used this opportunity to share the celebration and strengthen the community links. Making these allowances is a practice of equity, it ensures the inclusion of all children into events, as well as giving value to family life and religion. Family and spiritual life was vital to Froebel (Froebel, 1826, 1899; Lilley, 1967). He knew that educating the whole child included the religious, spiritual and family values that each child would hold. By recognizing and celebrating these, Froebelians enable children to develop their whole sense of self.

More implicitly lies the tensions that permeate within education settings. One educator set up a café for the children to access as part of their role play. This was unfamiliar to the children who had not experienced this themselves, having only visited fast food chains with their families. Only by recognizing the reality of the lives of the children in the setting can educators ensure that what they offer to children provides them with an experience that is related to their own, and new experiences are offered through trips and visits. One educator brought in resources to be used in a hair dressing shop, as children were pretending to attend the barbers and using Lego pieces to be the clippers, standing for objects from their own experience. The educator was mindful of including creams, combs and hair products which all the children would have experienced in the hairdressers as well as including afro combs and beads for children's braids. By recognizing the reality of the children's experiences, they were able to invite others into this world. Froebelian educators use the term taking children from the 'known to the unknown' demonstrated in the hairdresser role play context.

In some communities such as the Gypsy, Roma and Traveller community, nomadic families may attend early childhood settings for periods of time. Educators need to be aware that, even in this short time, they still have a right to education and require support that is unique to their development and learning. Working with families from these communities may be time-sensitive and so practicing equity would demand that these children are prioritized and supported alongside regular communication with families.

When working with babies and young children, Sakr (2024) explores the ways in which rights and equity are maintained through routine practices such as sleep, intimate care and mealtimes. The Froebelian concept of freedom with guidance is applicable here, this involves the educator in guiding babies and young children in these routines whilst also ensuring rights are held, such as dissent for nappy changing, and finding ways to provide this care without causing distress.

Harry (aged six), a neurodivergent child was struggling to attend the setting on time due to his irregular sleeping patterns. The staff discussed a later start time could accommodate his needs. This supported the family, and enabled Harry to attend when he was ready. As everyone does, children can also struggle with good days and not so good days, particularly those with neurodivergence. Josiah (aged four) who seemed to be struggling with separation from parents and attendance, left the educators feeling stressed and exasperated with how to support him. They saw how Harry had a later start time and suggested this for Josiah. In this case, the educators needed to adapt practice by reviewing relationships, routines, environments and transitions to support Josiah effectively.

In one situation, like Harry's, the adaptation supports him in attending the setting, whereas in another this can be exclusion. Done et al. (2021) explore the 'endemic' of exclusionary practices in education systems across the globe, citing that those with additional needs and disabilities are often victim to these practices. In these situations, an accumulation of ineffective support can lead up to the point of exclusion. These include educator attitudes and perspectives, with a lack of leadership and appropriate support provided in the right place at the right time.

Within educational landscapes the quantitative discourse focuses on outcomes and data driven results which can alter the priorities through the system (Done and Andrews, 2020). A Froebelian perspective urges educators to return to valuing the child and understanding who they are and finding out what they need (Whistler and Montgomery, 2024). It is important that educators are working within the frameworks of the law and for the UK this includes the Equality Act 2010 and using the United Nations Convention of the Rights of the Child (UNCRC) to ensure that all children are able to access education as it is within their right to do so.

Approaches to enable equity within institutions

Racial tensions within education settings can be seen through statistics which depict a disproportionate number of teachers from those racialized as Black or Brown compared with white counterparts and is often paired with a social class-based advantage (Gorard et al., 2023; Titley, 2023). This draws attention to the possible barriers that may be in place for these groups, looking at structural racism as a cause for educator retention and recruitment (Grooms et al., 2021). Having educators and leaders who identify within these racial categories supports recognition and affirmation for children, families and educators of the same race. Yet, these educators must not be relied upon to lead on anti-racism without the holistic support from all those within the setting. Abrams (2019) discusses the inaccessibility of leadership positions for racialized groups within educational contexts, questioning ‘does my face fit leadership?’. Tembo et al. (2025) interview a Black headteacher describing the nineteen-year delay in her promotion due to the structural racism that she was victim to. The racism that occurs between educators and colleagues can also feed into practices with children. In one network of educators, the leaders were asked to review the end of year data through multiple lenses to watch for any patterns which would be detrimental to children from social categories such as race, gender and ability.

These divides raise questions as to how equitable the systems are and how educators are supported in their roles. It asks whether networks and specialized support for those experiencing discrimination exist and how to overcome these barriers. The South Asian Educators Network (SAEN) was created to support educators to provide a space and community of those with shared experiences. Within these meetings, there was a sense of collective empowerment, and being supported by others acting as guides, coaches and mentors for each other. Finding these spaces for community within education is vital to support the well-being of educators. This network identifies race and ethnicity as a common ground, however networks such as Early Education, Organisation Mondiale pour l'Éducation Préscolaire (OMEP) and The Froebel Trust enable early childhood educators to come together. Belonging to multiple networks reflects the concepts of diversity.

The tradition of networks continues through the Froebel gathering which is held annually in Roehampton, UK and online and brings together a celebration of all the Froebelian work within the UK and beyond. The International Froebel Society holds a conference every two years to present research and practice from all over the globe. These networks enable a community of practice which bolster ideas and empower educators to widen understanding and strengthen practice (Bruce, 2019; Bruce and Hunter, 2019). Bruce (Unity in Diversity, 2025) discusses how during Froebelian training, teachers were asked to find their speciality or interest and develop this. This is because Froebel wanted educators who were knowledgeable and, even though the role is holistic and educators need to be experts in child development, he knew the importance of having committed educators within their field. When there are dedicated teams within educational settings, the likelihood of quality and creative teaching increases. These specialized interests were embodied by Rosalie Lulham who lectured at the Froebel Educational Institute developing a nature study department (Bruce et al., 2019).

Considering global systems and institutions, Fiske and Ladd (2004) reflect on the creation of an education system in post-apartheid in South Africa. They discuss the challenges in changing ideas, status and power redistribution. A fundamental transformation was required by the South African government to address the inequality that the apartheid system imposed. Utilizing Critical Race Theory, which looks to transform the relationship among race, racism and power, offers a lens and tool to interrupt inequity and inequality in the system. (Adonis and Silinda, 2021; Delgado and Stefancic, 2023: 379). Ngubane and Makua (2021a, 2021b) explore Ubuntu pedagogy, an indigenous African philosophy as a means to transform the educational practices in South Africa. This alternative lens provides a decolonial approach that fundamentally supports social justice and inclusion and provides a hopeful perspective which aligns closely to Froebelian principles of connection and unity.

The wider context of the UNCRC or Universal Declaration of Human Rights (UDHR) may be adhered to in principle, however in practice it may be quite different. Working towards these concepts of equality through equitable working holds at the forefront the need for fairness and justice to all individuals and communities. Within the educational context, the UNCRC is sometimes woven into curricula, perhaps in a superficial way which loses meaning over time. Continuously renewing and reminding educators and teams of the rights for children adds gravitas and wider contextual reasoning to the role of the educators. This way of working, helps to transform the systems and contexts in which individuals work.

The four freedoms

Achieving equality within the educational context can be framed around the four freedoms. These were developed by Eleanor Roosevelt (2012) and align with the UDHR to promote the connection of nations across the world. The four freedoms provide a framework through which to explore and emancipate educational practice towards a socially just framework. These freedoms from fear and want, and of speech and worship, enable a more holistic foundation to provide actionable steps to enable social justice within education.

Remaining critical of the sources that are used to form these frameworks is a reminder to be aware that they arose from a singular viewpoint and from a period in history which is different to society today. Puntambekar (2023) discusses the concept of human freedoms which transcend political aspirations and focus on spiritual, social and moral concepts of freedom (see Table 5.1). There are similarities to Furman's (2012) dimensions of social justice, particularly when looking at holism and the interconnectedness of humanity. These concepts require comprehensive consideration of what it means to be a human in this world today. In Froebel's time there was a heavy influence from indigenous practices around the world through colonialism and trade in India and China (Williams, 2003). Potentially absorbed into the time and place, Froebelian ideas align closely to the emphasis on connections between mind, body and nature which can be seen in Hinduism, Buddhism and Taoism.

Enacting social justice comes in the form of access for all, participation from all and action to remove barriers and inequalities. The freedoms propose a pathway to listen, challenge and examine social justice within the context of educational settings. The freedoms can be applied to Froebelian education.

Freedom from fear draws a discussion around war, conflict, gangs and ways for settings to create safe spaces. Hill (2022) discusses how fear can be used as a commodity for those seeking to achieve power. This causes fragmentation and becomes ingrained through generations. It capitalizes on what is unknown and creates mistrust of difference and change. Froebelian principles of knowledgeable and nurturing educators counter this fear through encouraging relationships and bonds with children and families.

Freedom from want discusses physiological needs such as, shelter, sustenance, clothing and financial freedom. Situations for families can vary impacting on what is needed to live a fulfilling life. The freedom from want can be countered through Froebel's emphasis on children's autonomy and providing ways to support their decision making within their contexts.

Freedom of speech explores communication and expression. It examines different hierarchical standpoints which enable individuals to share their viewpoints. Froebel's ideas around freedom of speech can be applied in his ideas about symbolism

Table 5.1 *The Use of the Four Freedoms Go Hand in Hand with the UDHR, the UNCRC and the Human Freedoms. The Table Below Highlights the Connections Between the Different Frameworks*

Freedoms (Roosevelt, 2012)	Human freedoms (Puntambekar, 2023)	United Nations Convention of the Rights of the Child UNCRC (UNICEF, 1989)
Freedom from fear	Freedom from violence, freedom from exploitation, freedom from violation or dishonour, freedom from early death and disease, freedom from fear and frustration or despair	Article 11, 19, 33, 34, 35, 36, 37, 38, 39, 40
Freedom from want	Freedom from want	Article 6, 24, 26, 27, 28, 29,
Freedom of speech	Freedom of thought and conscience	Article 12, 13, 14
Freedom of worship	Absence of intolerance, compassion or fellow feeling	Article 7, 31

Table 1: Grouping freedoms, human freedoms and UNCRC

and representation. Reading, writing, drawing, dancing, music, role play are all forms of expressing oneself.

Freedom of worship is posited through spirituality, nature, cultural beliefs, rituals and songs. It reminds individuals that these aspects are foundational for humanity. This freedom is steeped within Froebelian education; his ideas of spirituality embody an education that is holistic, that supports children in connecting with their consciousness and sense of self. It takes on the Froebelian idea of the forms of life, beauty and knowledge; through appreciation of relationships, nature and the world around. This layer of freedom emphasizes a collective culture and community.

These freedoms are interwoven with each connecting to another. Without all of them together social justice cannot be achieved, however one doesn't necessarily come before another. A deeper exploration of these freedoms is explored in later chapters.

Critical thinking and advocacy

Educators have a pedagogical responsibility to support the needs of the children and families they work with. Settings, institutions and frameworks must be in place to support educators in carrying out their role effectively. The need for educators who are critical thinkers, knowledgeable and qualified supports children's development and learning. Those who are less experienced or without qualification need robust systems to be in place which provide pathways for developing critical consciousness within their practice. Supporting children and educators' ability to think for themselves, question and reflect on their practice, works towards a socially just educational context.

Froebel's way of promoting his ideas through various means included: writing in a newspaper about 'psychological and philosophical justification' of his approach to education, his commitment to training new teachers for his institutions, and his pursuing the role of women in education. He championed the use of networks, providing space for community and connection which has continued today. His articles were constant reminders to the community of the child and their right to play and ways in which families could support their children's learning. His critical thinking of the systems and ability to argue for change fits within the frameworks of social justice and reflection and action based on later Freirean principles.

The current frameworks that surround Froebelian education determined through a study of his writing and understanding his vision includes ten common principles (Bruce, 1987, 2015). These are continually explored and applied by those who embody Froebelian education in their current settings, as well as later iterations by Tovey (2017) and the Froebel Trust (2021). These principles act as a guide when working towards social justice.

CHAPTER 6

Freedom from Fear

Children who are ruled by fear experience an interruption in their normal development (Hyder, 2005). This means it is imperative for educators to reflect on how they can adapt practice to relieve fear from the social justice dimensions of which they have control.

The feeling of fear is a vital yet visceral feeling that is a survival mechanism ingrained in our brain which reacts to threats. The experience of a threat is determined by appraising the potential harm within a situation. This can be both conscious and unconscious (Ellmers et al., 2022). The human brain is not always able to differentiate between perceived threats.

The stress of a threat brings out a feeling of fear. These feelings can cause reactions to everyday things, such as a fear of unknown people, of the dark, spiders, small animals or sudden noises. To respond and relieve this and achieve a freedom from fear requires an interrogation of the different personal, cultural and political situations that enable fear to exist. Knowledge, information sharing and education are ways to develop understanding of situations in order to control and relieve the feelings of fear.

For example, Theo (aged four) was continually soiling himself in his new class which was not usual for him. Theo's family and the educators discussed altogether and it transpired that Theo was afraid of the loud noise of the dryer and walking to the toilets which were at the end of the corridor. To resolve this, hand towels were offered and an adult was on hand to walk with him to the toilets. This helped Theo to regain a sense of control of the situation. Eventually Theo was confident going to the toilet independently. When children experience fear that impedes on their physiological needs, little learning can take place. The educators and parents who were attentive to his needs were able to notice a pattern, ask questions and resolve the situation. Empathy is vital too as this enabled the educator to walk in the shoes of a four-year-old frightened of loud noises and a long corridor.

Froebel's writing may not have explicitly discussed fear but his concepts and worthwhile ideas for education can be connected to many of the ways in which educators support children in their settings. One of the underpinning concepts of Froebelian education is the understanding of the parts that make up a whole. He writes about how children's encounters in the world support their thinking of each thing as an 'undivided whole', as well as how it is organized as a part for a wider whole (Froebel, 1826: 91).

Risk-taking

The feeling of fear is linked with survival. Physical and bodily situations that bring about fear might be seen when children are taking risks such as on climbing frames. Having this sense of fear prevents unnecessary risk-taking. It can encourage children to take better managed risks considering the perception of their body. Sometimes educators and families are close by when children are taking risks. Their own fear can take over and may remind children to be careful because the adults themselves are fearful of the child falling. The feeling of fear is passed on. Children eventually internalize these messages. This sometimes helps children in being more careful but can also hinder appropriate risk-taking as being 'careful' might not mean anything to the child in their context (Tovey, 2007).

When educators feel unsure about children managing risks, they need to have a level of awareness of this and find their own ways to control what they can. In practice this might be asking a more risk-confident colleague to support children on the climbing frame until they feel more comfortable. Educators need to know that being specific and taking the time to explain to children what to watch out for and how to manage the risk is important, such as asking children how they have thought about coming off the climbing frame. Bringing awareness and enabling children to manage risk themselves removes the conscious feeling of fear, providing empowerment and control. Educators could be supported through planning and considering all risks through thorough risk assessment processes which may mitigate the feelings of fear. For example, considering how to manage cooking with young children by having rules of how many children are able to cook at once, or rules for using the overhead ladders (monkey bars) such as one-way paths and turn taking. Leaders need to ensure their teams are clear in how to support children appropriately when using equipment that is risky, by using provided guidance and their knowledge of children's strength and coordination development (Children's Play Advisory Service, 2020; Tovey, 2007). When educators are unsure, it can affect children's ability to develop their physical risk-taking skills. For example, Joseph (aged four) wanted to have a go at the overhead ladder and Michelle the educator helped him across by holding his bodyweight. This gave Joseph a false sense of confidence and safety in crossing the overhead ladder. Next time, he decided to go by himself, but found that he was not able to hold his own weight, so he fell off. Now Joseph was unsure of how to manage the risks himself and unaware that he needed to develop his own strength in holding his body first. Michelle needed to know how to support him appropriately on the equipment and an understanding of where too much support can hinder children's ability to manage their own risk, strength and coordination.

In Froebel's writing he emphasizes the exploration of outdoors, nature and the wider landscape, which can come with various risk-taking and risky play (Bruce, 2021). In exploring physical risks children begin to trial with materials asking 'what if I jump from here' and gaining a respect for their own body as well as nature which holds and receives them. He specifically writes about children climbing trees to gain new perspectives and see the landscape from a heightened view (Froebel, 1826). Froebel wanted children to explore with their whole body and test its limits. He knew that children's bodily autonomy is empowering and wrote how children shouldn't be hindered by 'too much assistance' (Froebel, 1826: 21). Froebel's concept of 'freedom with guidance' is important here.

Predictable environments

For young children who attend settings, there may be some familiar things that they routinely expect, which eases them into the space. For example, if paint is only out occasionally then children are drawn to it to explore it in many different ways, such as getting paint on their hands, covering paper with paint and using lots of paint resulting in wet paper. When paint is available each day, children are able to return to it at their own time and pace knowing that it will be there the following day to continue their exploration. This allows a deeper understanding of the resource and children are able to use it for their own creative purposes. Having a predictable environment enables children to feel settled and in control of their choices within the environment.

The environment is an important part of Froebelian practice, ensuring that there are regular, predictable resources available for children to explore (Adams and Short, 2025). This chimes with Bruce (1987, 1996, 2021) network for learning which has four interconnected aspects: the importance of first hand experiences, games with rules including cultural contexts, symbolic representation and play which coordinates the learning. The network for learning foregrounds Bruce's (1987, 1996, 2021) twelve features of play, and is further explored as layers of play in Pascal et al. (2026). For children to be able to learn, they need regular experiences with resources that develop their knowledge and mastery of the materials they are exploring. Educators need to understand what they are observing in children's play. This means knowing the development of children and what different play might be telling them, and being able to respond by offering further support or extending their play. When educators notice patterns in children's exploration, such as when they cover their paper in paint, they may realize it is an envelopment schema that is being explored (Athey, 1990; Louis, 2008, 2023). When educators know what to look for and can make sense of what they are observing, they can offer children different ways to explore this schema with a range of materials such as helping to wipe tables after lunch, or helping to clean large chalk boards with paintbrushes.

Having predictable adults in the room can support children and staff. For example, when there are absences, this has a huge impact on the children who feel unsettled with a substitute educator who may not know the children or the regular routines. In one setting there was a job share between educators, meaning that Harry was in for three days and Pam was in for two days. They knew the impact this would have on the children and displayed photos of who was going to be with them that day. Children relied on this heavily, and if this was not updated, they quickly updated this themselves. The feeling of knowing who is in the classroom can ease fear or uncertainty.

The settling in and transition of children into educational settings and nurseries can be a particularly fearful and upsetting time for children and families alike. Manning-Morton (2024) discusses how young children often don't understand why they are being separated from their adults. Developing a clear plan and ensuring that there is a personalized approach for each child and their family is important in removing the fear and worry that children have. Parents to twins, Romeo and Lucas (aged three), noticed how their behaviour changed when they approached the setting. The children began to display feelings of fear and anxiety. The educators were able to carefully respond to the children and slowed down the settling in process to ensure that they all felt comfortable. The parents attended more stay and play sessions, ensuring the same key person was present and playing alongside the twins. With all these strategies in place, they began to develop a 'triangle of trust' with their key person in the setting (Goldschmied and Jackson, 2004; The Froebel Trust, 2013). Eventually, they began to settle in and enjoy attending the setting. Focusing on the relationships that needed to be developed enabled a successful settling in process.

One way to establish relationships into systems within the setting is the use of key person approaches. The key person approach provides children and families with one or two people in the setting who they develop a relationship with and who to direct any questions, concerns or discussions about their child to (Goldschmied and Jackson, 2004). By having a group of children that the educator will work with closely throughout the year ensures that the relationships with children and families are meaningful and authentic. When these systems are established, routines such as home visits, parent consultations, book changing and daily discussions can be easily managed by the educators themselves. This removes any form of confusion and provides clarity, safety and assurance to children and families which enables the development of the triangle of trust.

These relationships are key to children feeling safe and secure in the setting enabling development and learning. Laevers and Moons (2008) developed the Leuven Scales of well-being and involvement which educators use with descriptions for the five different levels. Educators scan and screen the children's engagement in the learning environment and explore possible strategies to implement through the environment, interactions and relationships between families and between peers to improve children's well-being and involvement. Laevers and Declercq (2018) align the scales with supporting the commitment to children's rights through active listening and observing of children's well-being and involvement. Lucas and Romeo's setting were able to utilize this scale and noticed that the score of well-being was low and the steps they took to work with the family to improve this showed an improvement in their well-being at a later date.

Each of these examples discussed how enabling a sense of autonomy for children and educators can remove the feeling of fear from situations. There is a fine balance between having control to remove fear, and using control to create a false sense of security such as removing risks altogether. Highlighting the necessity of fear in situations to enable appropriate risk-taking instead of risk averseness is important. The examples have also demonstrated the need to continually reflect on the situation. Having blanket rules is not always appropriate as this removes the need to understand the nuances of fear within different situations and the different personal experiences of children and families (Keegan, 2024).

Overcoming fear within relationships

Relationships in educational settings enable children to feel safe and comfortable with educators. The systems within the setting need to prioritize and enable this to relieve children from fear. When Alina (aged two) joined the setting, her mother Mel was unsure of the educators who were working with her. Mel, who was a young parent, would avoid conversations at the beginning of the settling-in period. The leaders who discussed parental involvement with the educators suggested how they might support Mel in engaging with the setting. Building on the work of Athey (1990) who discussed how illuminating practice can support families in being involved in their child's learning and can empower and encourage them to engage with the setting, gave the educators ideas for supporting Mel and Alina. Over time, they managed to find moments with Mel to discuss Alina's interests and what they had noticed she had played with or was interested in during the school day. The educators asked questions about how Alina played at home, so Mel could share what she had observed. Mel began to feel more comfortable around the educators as they discussed Alina's learning as a focal point. Eventually, Mel shared that her initial apprehension with engaging with the setting was due to having met many professionals who discounted her due to her age. She was regularly judged for being a young parent and seen as incapable of parenting well. The approach the educators took enabled a collaborative relationship.

The power dynamic that educators and professionals hold can be daunting for parents particularly those who are vulnerable or marginalized. Knowing that relationships take time to nurture attests to the priority it needs to be given in settings. Relationships may not always develop positively straight away, and often a gentle, responsive and consistent approach to nurturing those relationships aids in developing a holistic picture to understand the child and family better. One of the foundational Froebelian principles include the importance of relationships (Froebel Trust, 2021). This includes relationships with educators and parents and between educators and children. Froebel also discusses the importance of a child's relationship with themselves (Froebel, 1826, 1861). This can lead to higher well-being and involvement in their learning. Alongside children's own sense of self, the relationship between educator or key person and family member is important for the child to observe. When Elinor Goldschmied's (2004) 'triangle of trust' is established, this can ease children's fears about new adults. By trusting the educators, parents implicitly give permission for children to trust them too.

Violence and fear

The reality of many familial situations can be challenging where there is domestic violence, sexual abuse and violence or communities that are run by gangs or afflicted by war. The seminal work of Hyder (2005: 100) reflects on the impact of war and conflict on children's development and learning and the 'crucial role of play in restoring lost childhoods and as a child's right'. She centres play as a way to support children and families who are experiencing violence and relies on supportive, knowledgeable educators to help relieve this fear. In these situations, educators need to find what they can control to help children and families find a space of relief. For example, in Palestine, there have been organizations which have found ways to maintain education whilst in temporary accommodation (Gaza Great Minds Foundation, 2025). Educators continue to work in dire situations to find ways to provide a sense of normality and routine for children. Children who are fleeing from war and conflict also have a right to education and play. Collaborating with others and creating a sense of community even in difficult circumstances can provide a short relief from fear which enables some sort of normalcy for children, families and educators all in the same situation.

Sometimes children who experience domestic violence at home, find the regular routines at a setting to be comforting as the spaces that are created by educators provide calm when there may be chaos elsewhere in a child's life (Manning-Morton, 2024). The opposite could also be true where children can find the boundaries and routines in a setting to be difficult to manage and behave violently. Educators need to know how to manage this in a supportive way. Behaviours are unique to children's experiences and there may not always be a clear solution in supporting them. Educators need to remain consistent and firm whilst also nurturing to support the expression of this frustration. Children may represent their experiences and ideas through who they become in their role-play and how they behave. Children's first hand experiences can be seen through observing their play (Bruce, 1991, 2021; Louis, 2023). When children witness atrocities committed using violence, weapons or war an educator may see play that can be quite uncomfortable, particularly if the play re-enacts what children have witnessed (Holland, 2003; Hyder, 2005; Paley,

1984). Violence and weapons create a false and misguided idea of safety as they create and depend on fear to exert control and damage to others. An educator observing in this situation may be unsure how to respond; Hill (2022) discusses when searching for the antidote to fear there must be a confrontation of the fear – facing it and preparing for it. This relies on the relationships that the educator has with the child and family, to begin to empathize with their situation and to be able to understand that their behaviours are an outcome of their circumstances. Finding out about the world of the child is vital in ensuring that fear is removed and a sense of empowerment and autonomy is offered where possible. Children who demonstrate violent behaviour may require further support in processing and self-regulating. If an educator is aware that loud noises disturb a child's feeling of safety, then fire drills or slamming doors mean that the educator must be ready to support this child through co-regulation. Eventually, the child may be able to regulate for themselves when they hear a loud sound, being able to understand that they are not in danger.

Looking at a child's life as a whole enables educators to see how the setting is a part of their life. Educators need to find out what children's realities are like. This can help in starting with where the child is, and encouraging them to explore their interests and needs within this stage (Louis, 2025). Louis and Betteridge (2024) ask whether educators look for children's good intentions debating whether educators are skewing their observations with bias or whether observation is based on curiosity and empathy for the child. Gemayel (2024) and Hyder (2005) describe how children will draw on positive play experiences in challenging times and how play can be used as a starting point to enable an understanding and relief from fear.

There are education-related social justice issues which are situated in the broader social, political, economic and environmental contexts. Utilizing self-reflection guides educators in assessing, critiquing and transforming the system where possible. These transformations may be on micro- or macro-scales. It is important to remember how each part is connected, building on Froebelian ideas of unity and connectedness (Froebel Trust, 2021). When there is a collective action towards social justice on whatever scale, the effects are felt when working directly with children. For example, in many settings in the UK there are lockdown protocols in case of an intruder on the site. These are not practised with the children in the same way as a fire drill might be. However, in settings across the United States there is a real fear of a possible school shooting which is prepared for due to the likelihood of this happening (Lee et al., 2022; Sandy Hook Promise, 2025). The interdependence of cultural, political and socio-economic situations causes various fears impacting children, families and educators.

Health and medical situations arising fear

Kyrie (aged three) had an allergy to milk and so the educators were quite fearful of having him close to the snack table where there was milk available for the children. They decided to adapt their snack time ensuring that he was offered fruit first and then anyone who wanted milk could come after to avoid cross contamination. This worked for a little while, but then his friends wanted to have milk so he missed out on sitting with them. The educators in the room reflected on the routine with Kyrie and his parents discussing whether he might be able to manage his allergy independently. This meant ensuring the children and Kyrie were all aware milk wasn't to go near him during fruit time. Kyrie was vocal enough to assert himself and educators were always present or close by. This solution relieved the fear from his parents and the educators, and empowered Kyrie in managing his health more independently.

Being inclusive is an important thread of education. Froebel emphasizes the need to start where the child is and continually reflect and adapt based on how children develop. Continuous reflection enables educators to re-evaluate, make changes and adapt based on the ever-changing and developing dynamics of the setting and building on their knowledge, understanding and relationship with children. Bruce (2004) writes, 'giving the right help, the right way, at the right time' which describes the role of the educator. Finding ways to support children's autonomy can remove the feeling of fear from classroom contexts. It is important to involve children in decision making such as consulting with them in appropriate ways to ensure their voices are heard in these processes. Froebel's writing discusses how he wanted his educational principles to help children to become autonomous, to think and take action for themselves (Bruce, 2021).

The COVID-19 pandemic bred a feeling of fear into the lives of everyone across the world. Many children and families became fearful of a microscopic virus that could be anywhere. Daily news reports kept updating the death toll, desensitizing the reality. One parent, Mark, mentioned that during this time his son, Jeremy (aged five), became very aware of death (Pascal and Bertram, 2024). Death had become so normal that Jeremy thought that he too would die soon. Mark was able to ease Jeremy's fears, explaining at an appropriate level ensuring accuracy but without sanitizing the truth. Like Jeremy, children are acutely aware of what is going on in the world around them. For children who have health worries and anxieties beginning to understand how viruses and germs work may provide a sense of empowerment. By knowing that there are germs that help us, and how to manage their health when they are unwell, like washing hands and coughing away from others, provides control over something that is unseen.

Navigating bereavement with young children can be difficult for all involved. Ongoing research by Rowland (n.d.) ensures active listening to children and families to ensure that there is adequate and appropriate support at these critical times. Child Bereavement UK (n.d.) discuss how some children will move in and out of their grief, and encourage families to use clear, accurate and age-appropriate language to discuss death.

Maternal mortality is an issue of systemic racism. In the UK the maternal mortality for Black women is almost four times higher than for white women (Toval et al., 2024; Women and Equalities Committee, 2023). A new parent and their child being discriminated against whilst needing medical attention can be a fear inducing double edged sword. Starting to address the fear by increasing knowledge, such as naming what is happening to Black mothers in childbirth, enables preparation and advocacy when facing these situations. This responsibility should not only fall to the mothers who are experiencing this but relies on health professionals in addressing their biases and being able to call out racist behaviour with colleagues.

If a child has been surrounded by fear and anxious adults, family members may also pass this onto educators when they attend settings. Relationships with family members are at the heart of social justice praxis and by understanding the prenatal and postnatal relationships as well as familial situations help the educator to see the whole child and family and begin to understand certain behaviours and observations. Focussing on creating and nurturing cultural contexts and family traditions through Elinor Goldschmied's 'Triangle of Trust' with each family can help to alleviate parental concerns.

Racism and fear

In the summer of 2024, the UK reported a number of 'anti-immigration protests' which stemmed from beliefs connected to race, religion and immigration (Downs, 2024). This led to rioting in areas across the UK, with news reports filming participants starting fires at hotels where refugees were housed. At the end of the summer, the riots quietened and many people involved in instigating, partaking or publicly agreeing with the protests and riots returned to their daily lives.

There are a multitude of layers within these events. First, the language used around the reporting of the incidents which were in the news called protests and colloquially called riots. The language used evokes different connotations to the rights of the individual. A protest would suggest a peaceful, fair rights-based event, whereas a riot suggests disorder and illegal activity. Second, due to the language used, the police deployed would have been acting differently – if it were a riot, theoretically there may be more force being used in stopping the incidents, whereas if it were a protest there are supposed to be more protective measures ensuring the safety of all involved. Finally, whilst arrests and charges were made, those who returned to their daily lives returned to their communities alongside those they may have been rioting against. The fear within the communities of those targeted was understandably heightened. The fear in this situation created fragmentation, isolation and mistrust in neighbours and friends. Those children, families, educators and colleagues who were targeted by and took part in the riots would have returned to work with each other and a sense of fear brought into the setting with it.

For families who had emigrated to the UK in the 1970s and 1980s, they were reminded of their childhoods which were marred with race riots and fear similar to what they were witnessing in 2024.

These situations cause further divides by creating a general sense of mistrust within communities and associating characteristics and demographics to those with certain viewpoints like in the 1970s when punk music was associated to National Front demonstrations (Worley and Copsey, 2016).

Tackling this in settings requires a critical discussion with self and others. Maintaining safety and relationships with children, families and educators whilst also knowing there may be discriminatory views within the community is challenging. Educators can address only what they know and observe. Countering prejudicial narratives which may be ingrained and fixed in many people, needs to take a gentle process that looks for commonality. For example, Jonah, a parent at a Christian school, mentioned to Rosie, a staff member, that he was uncomfortable with Tolu, an educator who wore a hijab, in his son's class. Whilst Jonah's views are inherently Islamophobic, lecturing him about this may make him defensive and abandon any possibility for discussion. Rosie, in an attempt to understand what he was thinking and where his ideas possibly stemmed from, explained more about Islam and its areas of commonality with Christianity; mentioning how many Muslim women dress modestly in clothing similar to nuns and how Jesus is mentioned in the Quran as a prophet. Jonah was able to engage in a dialogue with Rosie, and she was able to explain that having discomfort about something unknown was normal, but suggested that he might like to find out a little bit more before making judgements which can lead to discrimination. To change someone's mind there needs to be an exploration of understanding particularly trying to find out where these ideas might come from. Rosie had this discussion with Jonah but it would not be fair to burden Tolu with this. Lending empathy to those who have discriminatory viewpoints is very challenging. However, this has to be explored in order to understand the individual and to see the situation as a whole through a calm and rational discussion. Jonah's viewpoints may not have been changed entirely, but the dialogue is a starting point which may be a seed that eventually germinates.

Those who have prejudiced beliefs are also victims of fear. Fear rules the imagination and builds narrow viewpoints of individuals and communities, with news and media which confirms bias and the hierarchy of difference. Yet, centring those who are targets of the riots or discrimination is important in ensuring that their sense of fear is eased. They need to feel comfortable in expressing their identity and celebrating their diversity. In the early childhood setting this may look like ensuring that children, families and educators are not fearful of being themselves, and if there are prejudiced comments these are dealt with by patient educators who can explore where these viewpoints stem from, and offer alternative ideas that connect with the individual and enable compassion for others. Settings also need to prepare for incidents and events such as these by ensuring equality policies are embedded into practice (Lane, 2008).

Turning fear and despair into hope

Exploring fear can make educators feel helpless. An antidote to fear is grounded on access to knowledge and education, reasoning and being able to ask questions to widen understanding and context (Hill, 2022). In each of the examples explored in this chapter, the unknown plays a huge role in compounding fear, and the themes arising share a tension between ideals and limitations (Yılmaz, 2025). Being free from fear may not always be a reality, but for some, moments that ease fear can transform lives. In the early childhood context, educators can work with children and families to enable this freedom within their settings. By building on the relationships that exist within educational contexts, Froebelian pedagogy can support the collective transformation of the system in which educators are working within. Whinnett (2025) explores the idea of Froebel as a pioneer. He was a leader in his field connecting spirituality, education and philosophical concepts together, ultimately viewing children as essentially good. He highlighted the need for resilience, creativity and empathy in which fear can be dispelled and an alternative imagined.

CHAPTER 7

Freedom from Want

This chapter explores how freedom from physiological needs and accessing resources can be addressed within educational settings and governmental policies. Many families may experience violence, war, homelessness, living in temporary accommodation, hunger and financial situations that continually escalate. These are all varying degrees of 'want' or 'need'. Relationships, food, clothing and shelter affect the individual and relate to socio-economic systems within countries.

Sustaining and maintaining physiological needs are the basics required to live in society. Maslow's hierarchy of needs are one way of viewing freedom from want. They focus on the biological and physiological requirements needed to survive which motivates individuals to seek fulfilment of these needs (Maslow, 1943). Although Maslow's pioneering ideas are seminal, there is an underlying narrow perspective which focuses on hierarchy rather than interconnection, implicitly arguing that not all human needs are equally important. Looking at the needs through an interconnective perspective enables the multifaceted requirements to survive and thrive and to be seen as connected and interdependent. For example, without sustenance there is a low likelihood of survival, however, if there is food availability, but no feeling of safety, the likelihood of survival is not necessarily increased.

The Universal Declaration of Human Rights (UDHR) and the United Nations Convention on the Rights of the Child

(UNCRC) both state the need for individuals and children to have a standard of living that is adequate for health and well-being (UNICEF, 1989; United Nations, 1948). The terminology remains vague and it is up to different countries to decide what 'adequate' might be defined as. For the purposes of this book, freedom from want is about the child and family's right to have what they need to *thrive*. Surviving is about meeting basic needs in order to stay alive; thriving is about meeting the needs which bring the possibilities to have a healthy life and sense of well-being. In educational settings, children need to have some sense of well-being to be able to develop and learn, which can be supported by knowledgeable and nurturing educators.

A typical view is that those who require support to survive and thrive are responsible for their own situations. This attitude ignores the bias of individuals and hierarchies of difference that exist within communities and systems. Those who require freedom from want are viewed as 'less than' and marginalised or labelled as individuals who don't want to work hard. The narrative quickly spirals into lazy versus hardworking. There is a much more nuanced perspective for those who are deprived of their basic needs without categorising their situation into binaries. In 2024, 21 per cent of people experienced poverty in the UK, this equates to 4.5 million children, with this number increasing due to rising costs of living (Francis-Devine, 2025). The term 'cost of living' demonstrates the monetisation of an individual's survival, often rendering them to a number. This adds to the ever-present stigma of asking for help to be able to survive and to maintain dignity.

Food security

Food that supports children's health and well-being through a well-balanced diet enables development and learning. In the UK, most children bring or have a meal as part of the school day, including fruit and milk being available throughout the day. Sam (aged four) would sometimes take the fruit during snack time and hide under the table to eat this. His key person, Julie, questioning this behaviour, met with a colleague. They had worked with Sam's family and this behaviour was not unusual due to the scarcity of food at home. At home he and his siblings were hungry and were often not able to satisfy their hunger without fighting over food. Educators are not responsible for solving familial situations, however, understanding Sam's situation gave Julie an answer to his behaviour. She sat with Sam during fruit times to enable Sam's feeling of safety, and to reduce his stress around food. She ensured there was enough fruit for everyone and it was placed in a large transparent bowl so Sam and the other children could see the fruit and choose how much they wanted without needing to hoard or hide. Sam eventually learnt that he was safe to eat his food with his peers and that his food would not be taken from him. This slow, gentle approach, similar to Clark's (2023) work on slow pedagogy enabled Sam to settle .

Slow pedagogy chimes closely with Froebelian pedagogy (Froebel Trust, 2022). Froebel's ideas on unhurried approaches connect with the idea of freedoms. Liebschner (1992) discusses the concept of freedom in Froebel's time as connected to children's participation of learning, trying to be free from the transmissive model of education. Children's freedom to play enables and coordinates their learning, so time which is free from unnecessary interruptions enabling a flow of the rhythm and routine of the setting can help children to feel more settled and engaged in their own development and learning. The concept of 'being with' which Clark (2023) describes as 'lingering' and 'listening' was embodied by Julie in the example.

Julie brought her observations to meetings, and this began discussions in the Nursery about their practice. They had observed that they had been using food in the environment for children to play with. On reflection, they decided that they would no longer use food for play. They felt that it was disrespectful to use food in this way particularly as many of their families relied on the food bank. The team also realised that it was confusing to play with food, creating rules that food which was played with cannot be eaten, but the same food might be served later at lunch. By sharing with her colleagues, Julie was able to engage in a reflective dialogue about her practice. This enabled further reflection with other colleagues who in turn made changes to their practice.

Rich discussions of issues, problems or observations enable a critical pedagogy that develops educators in their work towards a socially just setting (Elfer, 2024; Freire, 1970; Louis, 2023; Pascal et al., 2026) This example demonstrates how one observation and an educator's professional curiosity cascades into a series of reflections that brought together the settings ideas on how they use food and to enable a freedom for Sam and any child in their setting who are concerned about access to food. As Bruce (2021: 112) states, 'Froebel's writings show his attention to observation'. Interpreting observations helps educators to understand children and find appropriate ways to support and extend children's learning. Louis (2023: 75) warns however, that 'interpretations are not neutral or value-free – they are influenced by our lived experiences, values, beliefs, culture and professional knowledge'. Ensuring that this is held in mind throughout educators' observations can help to achieve equality within the setting. Discussing observations with colleagues can deepen understanding, change perspectives and intensify curiosity. Freire (1998: 81) writes, 'Curiosity is what makes me question, know, act, ask again and recognise.' This process builds on his understanding of authentic reflection followed by action (Freire, 1970).

Collaborative projects to enable food security

One setting was closely linked to a local food bank. They left donations outside the gates for families to choose but found many families didn't take from it. The leader of the setting, spoke to the families to find out why. They realised the issue was multifaceted. Families felt embarrassed taking the food and they didn't know what to do with some of the produce. The offering of the food created a power and status imbalance, with families feeling 'less than' when being seen taking from the donations. And it highlighted the different experiences of cooking that many families were not as familiar with.

The educators responded by establishing regular sessions for 'cook offs' with the donated produce and the produce grown by the children in their garden. Children and families would cook food in the afternoons. They were reminded of recipes from their own cultures and experiences, sharing how easy it was to cook a variety of food with simple ingredients. Over time the group began to grow and become more cohesive. This enabled a more empowered and independent community built on what they *can* do instead of what they were lacking in. If there had been an alternative approach which focussed on what the families were embarrassed or not aware of, the power imbalance between those who 'knew' about food and cooking and those who didn't could have created further fragmentation of the community.

The project evolved into developing the garden and creating space specifically for growing more produce. The children and families were all involved in this, and together they learnt about how to cultivate food that they would use in the 'cook offs' (Bruce, 2012; Froebel Trust, 2024). The children's plants grew so well that they were able to donate back to the food bank, furthering the community cohesion.

Long-term investment into nurturing community creates ripple effects. All the children and families learnt about growing, harvesting and cooking food. Learning about the science of where food comes from, and the sustainable actions from seed to plate all impact children's relationship with food, and family's ability to engage in nature, cooking and develop healthy nutritional knowledge (Denton and Parker, 2024). Froebel saw nature as the ultimate teacher, which provided a huge range of experiences which aligned to nature's laws (Razzall, 2024). When children engage in nature, and help to cultivate plants for food, they are able to experience fully the life cycle as well as the circular process of composting. Froebel knew the importance of caring for nature such as plants and animals – including tiny ants; 'the child who has cared for another living thing, is more easily led to care for his own life' (Lilley, 1967: 129).

At each step of the process, centring long-term sustainable community cohesion rooted a positive relationship with food, and enabled freedom from want through empowerment and sharing of knowledge and experience. When Froebel wrote about community, he was thinking about the sense of belonging that is of utmost importance to a child and family's place in the community. Feeling like one who belongs, connects to Chapter 3 – finding others with similarities and differences. The project this setting undertook is not a blueprint that can be taken and replicated. The leaders of the setting ensured there was an active listening and responding to what the children and families needed and wanted. To enhance community cohesion, the setting needs to actively listen and take action which will bring together the relationships and place it on firmer more longer lasting ground for it to flourish.

Shelter and accommodation

During a home visit, Rachel and Asma visited Josephine (mother) and Laurenco (aged three) who lived in a rented room in a large house. The room had little furniture, and nothing for Laurenco to play with. Laurenco was looking at his mother's phone, whilst she lay in bed as she had been working a night shift. This observation of a family home is a reality for many children and families who are living in poverty and are unable to seek assistance for housing through social housing schemes and local governments. Housing crises in many cities are forcing families to pay extortionate rents yet still be living in unsanitary conditions (Tweneboa, 2024). Had Rachel and Asma not visited this family they would be unaware of what the life of this family was like. Home visits are one way of developing a holistic understanding of the child and family, they may not always be possible due to different housing situations. Holmes (2025) suggests utilizing 'third spaces' such as cafés, parks and local areas to meet children and their families before starting in a setting. Educators are not responsible for supporting the family with housing but are considered front-line workers and so Rachel and Asma were responsible for recording what they saw and to pass on information to early help teams and housing teams within the local government. They also were able to reflect on how they would be able to support Laurenco when he started at the setting. They spent extra time with him reading stories and providing opportunities for him to climb trees, jump in puddles and ride bikes. They encouraged Josephine to take short trips to the local park when she had a day off from work.

Children who are attending settings might live in temporary accommodation such as hotels, rooms in large homes with communal areas or women's shelters. Educators need to be sensitive and understand that children may require different support based on what they're experiencing. In Froebelian terms this would be 'begin where the learner is' which aligns closely to Chapter 5 – equity. The complexities of different familial situations may impact other areas of need such as Jason's family which was living in temporary hotel accommodation. His family had no place to cook food so needed to spend a large amount on takeaways, fast food or restaurants to ensure they weren't hungry. This left his family in huge financial difficulty which could have been avoided if there was appropriate accommodation with cooking facilities. The setting he attended was able to ensure Jason had a place in breakfast club and afterschool club which ensured he was getting most of his meals there which relieved the pressure for his family.

Educational institutions during Froebel's time were often founded through the context of religion. His school in Keilhau and his kindergarten in Bad Blankenburg pioneered secular inclusive education (Bruce, 2021). This type of education was open to all – rich and poor and those from different religions. Whilst Froebel's period would have had a narrow diversity, the sentiment of inclusive education still prevails. Through this type of education, educators are able to meet the children and families where they are at (Liebschner, 1992).

Relationships, friendships and well-being

How educators work with children and families can enable freedom from want. Especially through encouraging relationships and friendships between children and families, creating support networks in the community. Friendships within the setting enable children to learn and celebrate with others and share empathy. The need for authentic and meaningful relationships is intrinsic to human nature. Ensuring that there are opportunities within settings for friendships to flourish is important. Maguire and Dunn (1997) discuss how friendship develops children's play and emotional development. Bella and Seren (aged four) were good friends since nursery. They played with each other every day often role-playing or drawing and painting. Bella's family was relocated suddenly and so needed to move schools. Seren felt alone and shared with the educator how sad she was and how much she missed Bella. Some families are not aware of how changes in friendships can alter children's lives and learning. Whilst this was out of Bella, Seren and the educator's control, when these things do happen there could be a way of maintaining contact through video calls or letter writing. Educators may be able to encourage families to develop the bond between children, as this may also develop a bond between families. Froebelian principles connect deeply through relationships. These are vital for children and all humans to survive. Froebel believed that children learn about themselves through others including friendships that occur within an educational setting. These interactions help children to understand what they can do and what they like or dislike. They learn about negotiating and problem-solving, about holding other people's emotions as well as their own. These complex skills occur through play, when children are having to continually compromise and work out how they will maintain their play episode with their friend. The Scottish curriculum guidance 'Realising the ambition' and the Curriculum for Wales have children's well-being embedded into the frameworks (Scottish Government, 2020; Welsh Government, 2022). Both these frameworks build on relationships between children, educators and family members. Holding secure the emotional well-being of children is at the heart of this work, and both documents closely align with the overarching principles of the UNCRC, with Scotland having made them law (Scottish Government, 2024; UNICEF, 1989).

Uniform – freedom or restriction?

Freedom from want through the perspective of clothing and appearance is a rising debate within educational settings. Many settings may have uniform policies, dress codes for children and educators or a more general policy on appearance.

The UK Government (2024) outlines guidance to suggest to settings that any uniform policy should adhere to the Human Rights Act 1998 and Equality Act 2010. Ensuring that settings are considering the protected characteristics of any child and educator who the policy applies to. In addition, the guidance outlines cost considerations for families needing to purchase uniform and how this can be arranged through second hand shops and within settings. These seem to be sensible guidelines but still leave a setting to interpret them in their own ways.

In theory, uniform could enable equality and community by having all children wear similar colours and clothes. They enable children to 'mess up' their uniform instead of their own clothes from home. However this can also have an opposite effect where parents wish to keep the uniform pristine for it to last longer and keep up appearance. It can also cause further stress on families who have limited clothing or ability to clean and wash clothes quickly, which can quickly raise issues and non-compliance of uniform policies further highlighting the family situation. Settings can reduce this stress by asking for donations towards clothing banks within the setting or access to spare uniform to ensure children's dignity remains intact.

Wearing their own clothes, rather than a uniform, enables children's individuality and diversity to be celebrated. However, this could become quite expensive for families as they may need to purchase more clothing or there may be competition and shame based on branding and designer clothing. For example, Kamal (aged three) explained to Louie (aged three) that the 'tick' on his shoes made him run faster, and so Louie was convinced that he needed to get the same shoes. One way to reduce the costs for families is by only requesting children wear a school jumper and enable families to find their own options for items such as trousers and shirts from donations, or budget clothing shops. Increasingly, many clothing stores support a 'fast fashion' trend with low-quality clothing which can easily rip and tear as well as having an impact on the environment by increasing waste (Niinimäki et al., 2020). Yet, this might offer an opportunity for settings to develop sewing and weaving in their environments. By introducing a variety of ways to mend clothing by adding buttons or closing holes, children learn how to care for their clothing and develop a more sustainable approach (Imray et al., 2023).

Educators in one setting noticed that many families were unable to purchase clothing for winter or wet weather, so decided to purchase a set of 'welly' boots, waterproof and warm jackets. This enabled children to change into these clothes when they were outside, to stay warm and comfortable whilst being able to engage fully outdoors. A one-off purchase from the setting may be initially expensive, but as it is reused every year there are no further associated costs so this can be managed more easily.

Harding (2024) reflects on the museum at Froebel's first kindergarten in Bad Blankenburg. Here a piece of clothing that the children would wear whilst attending was of unbleached linen. During Froebel's time the linen industry was developing, which may have attributed to the use of this material as part of his uniform. Unbleached linen is easy to maintain, and requires more milder treatment to keep clean and dry. This most likely would have kept costs down for Froebel but also made the children who attended his kindergarten stand out, as this was opposed to much of the fashion influenced by the French Napoleonic era at this time. Froebelian education encouraged outdoor activity and learning therefore uniform needed to be appropriate to support this. The uniform attests to Froebel's idea of individuality and unity, whilst also nodding to the tensions between these as they do today.

The discussion on uniform requires further questioning and exploration as to why children's dress and appearance need to be dictated and controlled at all. This includes hair discrimination with some types of hair seen as acceptable and others not. This can often be a challenge for children with Afro hair types (Bragg and Ringrose, 2023). Biased gender narratives favour settings not allowing girls to wear trousers, and skirt lengths being measured adding to issues around sexualisation of young girls often associated with adultification of Black girls and higher levels of body surveillance (Grower et al., 2021). In one setting, Rowan's mother asked the educator about the uniform policy. Rowan (aged five) wanted to wear skirts to school but it wasn't clear from the policy whether this was allowed. This began a discussion with other educators and leaders about whether there should be a more gender-neutral uniform policy (End Sexism in Schools, 2025). Eventually, this was implemented and ensured all children were welcome to wear what they liked from the uniform list.

Financial freedom

When living and working in a capitalist society, the need for money and financial freedom enables an individual and family to be able to access what they might need to find freedom from want. It focuses on the individualistic responsibility to solve their freedom from want. This viewpoint maintains an isolated and fragmented perspective of society. Enabling financial freedom from a social justice perspective within an educational setting may look like ensuring there is fair access for funding for each classroom and department. For example, Amy, a teacher, bought her own books to the setting for the children in her class to share. Kezia from the classroom next door wasn't able to afford all these books so had to use what the school had provided. The children in her class were not able to access the same literature which created inequality. Amy could have shared with Kezia but as these were her books, she was more possessive of them. The school needed to review the books available and ensure there was an equality of access which did not rely on what the teacher brought with them. Included in educator training, resourcing a setting or a room can be done through low cost or completely free methods. This includes recycling, using found items such as conkers, pine cones and shells, using social media marketplaces where things might be given away for free, contacting local businesses and tradespeople to find unwanted items. When settings struggle with budget, there are a multitude of ways to find the right things for children to use. These have effects on the environment and connect to children's own experiences and communities (Gura, 1996).

Traditionally, the teaching profession is viewed as a predominantly middle class profession (Lampert et al., 2016). Whereas there is a drive to diversify recruitment of educators, the social class can alter relationships between children and families as well as between colleagues (Keane, 2024). This can create divisions as it did with a setting whose staff attended a social event on a Friday evening. There was a group of educators who preferred a more expensive venue, whereas others preferred a cheaper one. This created a divide which essentially became those who can afford and those who can't. Reflecting on this, the team decided to find a new venue that was preferable for all. They found a restaurant which was welcoming, inexpensive and was more inclusive to those who didn't drink alcohol. Finding ways to be inclusive to all enables a more cohesive community and fosters well-being for educators.

Navigating tensions in the freedom from want

A social justice perspective in a society driven by economics finds itself in a contradictory position (Kent, 2005). To work towards social justice, there are multiple paths to follow at the same time. One is to look at ways to dismantle and transform the systems to achieve freedom from want. Another is to work within the capitalist system by trying to achieve a financial freedom which can enable a freedom from want of other things. Another path is to find communities of resistance and aligned thinking which fosters social justice within smaller groups and focusses on the relationships between individuals and communities to find where there can be support for each other. All three pathways need to be followed and maintained at the same time.

McGarvey (2022) discusses the need for those with lived experience of difficult situations to support others who are currently experiencing them. Walking *with* others in their situation develops a sense of community, comradery and a sense of hope, whilst also having a humbling and empathetic ability to fully understand a situation. When there is a sense of community, individuals are responsible and accountable for their own lives and develop a reciprocal relationship to the community by contributing support for arising issues and struggles.

Charities and food banks are heavily relied on by communities and governments. Carr (2023) suggests that systems such as minimum national wage in the UK are not fair as they do not equate to what is needed to live in a high-cost society. A trial of a universal basic income showed the impact on decreasing poverty in London by 5.7 per cent (Mayor of London, 2023). According to Davis et al. (2022) a universal income would reduce barriers of access such as improving education, access to higher education and health benefits. Imagining a society where poverty and barriers are reduced is a pathway towards achieving freedom from want and social justice.

An early childhood setting in the township Soweto, South Africa had a high priority placed on providing breakfast and lunch each day, and for younger children, ensuring they were able to sleep. The setting prioritised these basic needs for the local families because this is what they needed. The educators also came from the township and so brought their mobile phones to charge as they didn't have electricity in their homes. When the children ate their breakfast and lunch, meals for the educators were also provided. In this safe place children and staff enjoyed their meals together. There was the Froebelian interdependence of nutrition for physical health and a feeling of community promoting healthy well-being. There are many tensions within freedom from want. It can easily become despairing particularly when there are situations out of an individual's immediate control. A Froebelian pedagogy and perspective enables educators to work within a frame that focuses on a principled approach to each problem or issue that arises. Having a clear frame can bring out positivity and hope from each situation. A Froebelian approach is a hopeful approach; maintaining this hope is vital in imagining a future which is socially just.

CHAPTER 8

Freedom of Speech

This chapter explores the freedom of speech within educational settings. Examining how listening, communication and language all impact this freedom through relationships within the settings, to wider systems, policies and societal structures that exist within languages, viewpoints and ideas. A final section discusses how expression is limiting. For example, spoken language or written words require adherence to rules. These are followed within cultural contexts to enact social justice through this freedom using stories.

Freedom of speech includes listening, communicating and using language and expression to make meaning and to be understood in the cultural context in which children live. Freedom of speech and expression within a social justice perspective understands that an individual's expression should be maintained as long as it is expressed peacefully and not infringing on the rights of another (Amnesty International, 2025). The United Nations (n.d) agree there must be protections in place which keep hate speech from escalating and ensure that access to fact-checked information is available.

The Rabat Plan of Action and its associated Rabat threshold test provides a framework in which to maintain freedom of expression and reduce restrictions where possible. The test outlines six parts: context of the statement, speaker's position or status, intent to incite audience against target group, content and form of the statement, extent of its dissemination and likelihood of harm (United Nations, 2012). This aligns closely to the idea of 'universal human ethic' which outlines an ethical responsibility for educators, and those whose work effect children's lives (Freire, 1998).

Interconnecting with freedom from fear and want, freedom of speech enables educators to find out what might be causing fear or want in children and families and to support them appropriately. Froebel advocated for children's education to be free and to enable free thinking. His ideas for a free-thinking institution were challenged by the government and this led to his kindergartens being banned. He wrote to the governing authority advocating for children's entitlement to a holistic education stating, 'Do not allow the matter of childhood to become a tool of political parties' (Liebschner, 1992: 30). This quote can be applied in today's world. Finding spaces for expressing and sharing viewpoints on education is an important aspect in following Froebel's footsteps and providing children with a holistic education.

Listening

The United Nations Convention of the Rights of the Child (UNCRC) general principles include the right to be heard (UNICEF, 1989). This implies active listening is needed from those who are enacting on behalf of children. When a setting listens to the feedback from the stakeholders such as governors, parents, educators and children, and responds effectively, they may demonstrate how they view the community and how they want to work with the community, including whether they stifle any criticism (Wall, 2024). Listening is one step, the next would be to reflect and take action similar to Furman's ideas of social justice and the Freirean concepts of critical pedagogy discussed in Chapter 3, Diversity (Freire, 1970; Furman, 2012).

When educators actively listen to children, this helps to create a holistic picture, and understand children's context and circumstances. Children's voices are different depending on their age. For babies and toddlers, listening may include observing expressions and gestures. When educators closely observe babies within early childhood settings their meaning making and intentions can be seen. Drawing attention to the inclusion of babies voices is increasingly viewed as 'morally essential' particularly within settings (Guard, 2023: 606). Building on these ideas, Sakr (2024) discusses how educators must view babies as people with rights, holding this in mind in the context of children's play, their care and hygiene. Sakr asks educators to question where they can enable babies to make decisions for themselves, and how these are expressed, listened to and responded to. Guard (2024) introduces the concept of 'Adagio interactions' which slow down the pace of the setting to enable interactions between baby and educator to materialize. This encourages active listening and responding aligned with intersubjectivity and attunement of young children (Trevarthen and Aitken, 2001). When listening closely most parents can differentiate between their baby's cry and that of others. This is something that educators working with babies learn to do quickly. For example, Leo (aged one) wanted to crawl from one side of the room to the other side but was continually picked up by Zak and placed back onto a carpeted area where there was no furniture. Educators need to carefully plan the space provided for babies to express themselves and develop physical and movement skills in the spaces they are in and organize the room from the literal perspective of the child (Davies, 2003; Guard, 2025). Leo eventually became frustrated and began to cry. He was not being supported in his self-determined learning which alerted Zak to changing his response. Instead of picking him up, he cleared a path to ensure that Leo was safe to crawl where he wanted to. Listening and observing baby's interactions with the space provided enables a reflection and response to support children's play. Froebel's last published work was the Family/ Mother songs (1844). The explanations included for each song provide great detail in how a family and baby engage and communicate with each other. He came to learn about children, relationships and their development and learning through observation (Bloch, 2024;

Louis, 2022). Froebel's study of children included the way babies and parents interacted together, movements of limbs and children's play.

Care and hygiene routines provide educators with opportunities to enable children's choices and freedom of speech. This involves thinking about who makes decisions as to what children will eat, how they eat and when they will have their nappy changed. Unnecessary handling of babies needs to be considered too, so that there is reflection about how educators physically interact with babies and infants. Ensuring that bodily care, handling and intimate care is undertaken *with* the children and not *to* the child (Manning-Morton, 2024; Sakr, 2024). Many educators might need to be making many decisions for babies, but valuing freedom of speech asks educators to be aware of the power and positionality they hold. Because settings need to manage multiple routines and factors when working with children, a slow pedagogy (Clark, 2023) and Adagio interactions (Guard, 2024) could enable time to be with children and listen to their needs, wants and thinking without the rush and haste of completing tasks. When leaders in settings reflect on how to facilitate educators in their active listening, there are minimal disruptions and uninterrupted time to respond effectively to the children they are listening to. Froebel implores educators to enable children's freedom. He writes 'a child will accustom himself to an environment when he has freedom of action and will be freely active where his surroundings are familiar' (Lilley, 1967: 101). This encompasses the role of the educator in creating an environment which encourages freedom to express themselves without rushing to the next routine. Froebelian educators strive to support children by encouraging their autonomy and thinking in their own time.

Active listening with families supports educators in working with their children and communicating children's development and learning. A partnership approach to working with families ensures that they are listened to and responded to appropriately. Educators need to reflect on whether families are overwhelmed with institutional requirements. For example, one parent, Sarah, shared how her three children attended a setting and she received three times the emails, often finding her inbox overloaded and unable to read or engage with what the setting needed. Sarah's feedback was heard by the leaders who reviewed how they communicated and streamlined information so that this was shared in multiple bite-sized ways that were more appropriate and helpful.

Consent and dissent

Daisy, an educator, came into the room and called to Elisa (aged two) who was playing, 'Come and give me a hug.' 'No' Elisa replied and returned to her play, Daisy acted offended. This interaction demonstrates the need for listening to children's speech, and enabling them to enact their wishes without judgements or influencing their decisions, particularly when it includes being handled or physical contact. Supporting children in expressing and maintaining their boundaries and personal space is of utmost importance in ensuring children's consent and dissent is followed. This includes interactions between educators and children and between children. Resonance, discussed in Chapter 3, Diversity, forms another perspective of consent and dissent through interactions. Elisa expresses repulsion which externally expressed through her dissent, is translated to Daisy adapting her response (Beljan, 2025). These daily interactions shape relationships and develop a sense of self and identity.

Children's dissent may be observed when educators are taking photos of their learning, sometimes children might glance at the camera, turn away or stop what they are doing to dissent from their picture being taken. Children become quickly aware of photos being taken, and might pose, or ask if the picture will be sent to their family. This topic is especially important to ensure active listening to children's expression of speech as there is an increase in photos of children shared on social media often without considering their wishes. Educators should discuss with families the policy of the setting, and how they enable privacy settings on their social media to ensure children's consent is upheld (Flewitt and Cowan, 2020; Quinn and Manning, 2013).

Often young children express their dissent through physical actions. Educators who know the children well, and have deep and meaningful relationships can support children in expressing their boundaries and aid them in negotiating a situation. Educators need to have understood the whole situation. For example, when Tanya and Melissa (aged four) argued and hit one another, Lauren the educator hadn't seen the whole interaction and tried to resolve this by asking the children to apologize. Lauren felt the situation was resolved, but both children were left frustrated and unsatisfied as there was no expression of the situation or the feelings the children had, nor was a solution negotiated. It also forced an apology when no one was apologetic. An opportunity for the leadership supporting Lauren would be to discuss co-regulation and understanding children's conflict. This could be through emotional validation, empathy and helping children to understand an appropriate expression of anger and frustration. Forcing children to apologize loses the meaning of the word 'sorry', as this becomes a word which holds absolution of any wrongdoing. It diminishes any opportunity to empathize and understand one another and enable children's moral development. The pedagogy of a Froebelian educator endeavours to trust children's intentions. Froebel writes how children may not always understand the consequences of their actions. Children need nurturing educators who enable them to see the impact of their action and develop their ideas of morality, right and wrong whilst understanding the consequences of their actions (Froebel, 1826).

The introduction or use of any behaviour policy or reward system that is used for public reward or humiliation can alter how children express themselves in ways they might seek to receive external rewards, rather than being helped to develop their moral framework and ethical understanding. Punishing children can be a humiliating and upsetting experience, children's ideas about right and wrong are developing so educators need to be sensitive and understanding of this – as a starting point considering themselves how it might feel to be publicly chastised. This is further confirmed by Trevarthen (2013: 5) who writes, 'a child who is ashamed does not learn new understanding, except how to avoid further humiliation'. Educators need to ensure that interactions with children are based upon mutual respect.

Rewards without specific meaning and context can alter children's motivations to make certain choices, perhaps choosing to help others to be publicly rewarded with stickers, instead of doing it through kindness and understanding. The effects of this can be seen when Ezekiel (aged four) saw that Harry (aged four) had hurt himself. He went over to Harry and asked if he was ok, whilst he did this Ezekiel looked for the educator nearby and repeated his question to Harry loudly hoping that the educator would hear, praise and reward him for doing the right thing. When the educator didn't respond, Ezekiel walked away leaving Harry. The ten common principles developed by Bruce (1987, 2021) built on Froebelian writing which emphasized self-discipline and autonomy. The intrinsic motivation to make moral choices supports children's self-discipline. Warneken and Tomasello (2014) further support this through their research which discusses extrinsic rewards and their undermining quality in supporting children's moral development.

Loud, quiet and silent voices

Educators need to be mindful of whose voices they are listening to and whose they may be ignoring. In busy settings there are multiple children's voices all seeking to express themselves sometimes all at the same time. There are also quieter voices who perhaps are not yet speaking or prefer to assert themselves quietly. Geri was being observed by her mentor Leah, who noticed that Geri responded to the children who were louder often demanding her attention. She reflected with Geri and suggested she video herself with a small group to see how she shared her attention. With this feedback and reflection in mind, Geri became more aware of the quieter voices in her class, and decided to spend more time listening to the children who seemed to get on with their chosen activities and play by themselves. Introducing systems such as focus children as described in Bartholomew and Bruce (1993) also supported Geri to ensure that there was a fairness of time spent with children throughout the school term.

The concept of bias, which was explored in Chapters 2 and 3, includes the different hierarchies of voices that are heard more willingly such as children who have an affinity with the educator (Louis and Betteridge, 2024). Rosemary noticed that she was spending more time with English speaking children because they were easy to communicate with. Reflecting on her bias, she ensured that she spent time observing and being with the children who didn't speak English. She realized that it was extremely important to spend time actively listening, observing and supporting these children as it would be much harder for them to express themselves as easily due to the language barrier. When she did, she noticed how Mariam created intricate items out of paper such as bags which she would cut tiny straps for, adding details and items inside her bag. Without these observations Rosemary would not have been able to find out what Mariam was interested in. Froebel emphasized observation of children's play to understand what children might be thinking and feeling. Louis (2022, 2023) builds on observation highlighting the need for educators to know what they are observing and making links to their knowledge of children's development.

Jaquiline and Daniel Sidney (2025) explore the increasing narrative in expecting conformity from children. This control is often related to how the educator is able to 'manage the classroom' and approaches which assume a transmission model of teaching (Bruce, 2021). These concepts view children as 'less than', taking away their own life experiences, knowledge and understanding. One way for children to express themselves is to be silent and refuse to take part or comply. This dissent clearly demonstrates how children feel and think about a situation. Children need to be heard and respected. The UNCRC explicitly states how children have a right to express themselves (UNICEF, 1989). Routines, systems and controls introduced to the setting by leaders or educators need to keep in mind children's voices in these matters. This can include how routines are implemented, how the classroom is set up, what is cooked for lunch and beyond. Including children in decision making enables children's thinking and reasoning. They begin to understand how they can contribute to their community and that they are being seen to contribute. Today in Froebel's school in Keilhau (Germany) children contribute through enterprise and self-governance. The building and systems support children in their self-governance through the regular chiming of the clock tower signalling the time. The chimes echo into the forest close by which is accessible without gates and fences and enable children to manage their own time and ensure they are present for their lessons (Joshi, 2023c). In settings, there are school council responsibilities which include eco-council and room monitors which provide children with a sense of belonging and purpose. These systems link closely to the Froebelian idea of 'freedom with guidance'. This term provides educators with an interactional instinct supporting reflection of whether to give more freedom or guidance. This is a scale which continually moves as children develop and learn (Liebschner, 1992).

Oracy and speech

Knight (2024) explores how oracy and cultural capital are closely intertwined with the emphasis on removing social inequality. The narrative often implies that those from marginalized communities such as working-class and racialized backgrounds are not coming from language-rich homes. Some oracy programmes encourage educators to correct children's spoken language by asking children to repeat and rephrase what they have said (Sherrington and Stafford 2018). In some settings there are curricula designed around 'word gaps' and behaviour policies which demand children's eye contact and body positioning. Cushing (2021, 2023, 2025) argues that these claims are flawed as they stem from deficit models which do not look at a broader perspective of social inequality. Oracy programmes depend on individualized and deficit models to experience upward social mobility, instead of considering the wider linguistic justice perspective. They offer a solution that seems to ignore the multitude of factors that have an impact on inequality and fail to consider the wider community, systems and ecological landscape of inherent inequality that contribute to individual lives.

Nair et al. (2023) add to this argument through the lens of speech and language interventions that many educators may be familiar with. The intention of these is to support children who are struggling with speech development. The authors argue that there is no wrong way of speaking, and those who uphold this narrative are not acknowledging the classist, racist and colonial knowledge base this stems from. The concept of 'standard English' refers to a specific academic ability, intelligence, confidence, manners and maturity of children (Cushing and Snell, 2023). These factors in turn suggest the limited access to resources and later implications of social mobility for the child and family. Programmes which police children's language and expression of speech need to be deeply reflected on and to explore whether deficit models are being enacted under the guise of social justice. This could include finding ways to develop children's spoken language whilst also celebrating their own home languages, or ways of speaking and performing perhaps through poetry, rap and songs. MC Grammar and Michael Rosen collaborate on retelling their stories through this media (Rosen, 2024). Introducing these approaches can create a more inclusive and meaningful context for speaking and language development. This aligns closely with Froebelian pedagogy which utilizes meaningful and purposeful contexts to provide a backdrop for learning that is relevant to the child.

Languages

It is important to keep in mind the different forms of communication that children may use or be introduced to. This includes the different languages spoken at home, signs that are used for British Sign Language (BSL) or Makaton. There are sometimes families who speak different languages at home who worry that their young child will not understand English so they stop speaking their home language. Whilst their intention is for their child to succeed in an English dominant society, they inadvertently reduce their identity, home language and mother tongue. Whitehead (2009, 2010) discusses how many young children might be multilingual and their contexts bring forward social histories and languages that transcend through generations, borders, time and space. This emotion that language holds deserves to be treasured by families and educators. The educator's role in supporting children's home languages is important for children's development of identity and sense of self. Bloch and Ellis (2021) add that emotions play a central role in cognitive functioning and speaking for young children. They continue by explaining the intrinsic need that all humans have to search for meaning and for belonging which children experience through play – a way of coordinating them both. For example, Mary (aged four) a fluent Spanish speaker often spoke to the children and educators in Spanish. Tom (aged five) only spoke English, but played with Mary building together with the blocks. She managed to balance the final piece in a precarious position. Tom congratulated her by saying 'Muy bien!'. This interaction demonstrates the experience of meaning making and belonging all through play. Encouraging languages and respecting them is important too. Educators can use home visits and settling in meetings to ensure that this information about the family is recorded and celebrated when children and families start in a setting.

Representative stories: Ways to express and belong

Being literate is many societies is an act of empowerment. The ability to read, write and engage with others through communicating can empower individuals in developing relationships, community and ensure they can advocate for themselves. Access to information, and being able to understand and respond to the information all links to levels of literacy.

Enabling children's communication, language and literacy can be undertaken holistically through stories, storytelling and story acting (Whinnett et al., 2020). Educators need to choose stories carefully, considering the different aspects of the book – the language, rhyming patterns, expression, storyline, illustrations and representation of children's lives and cultures. All stories may not be able to provide all of these aspects, but being mindful of what and how educators curate their stories is of high importance. Louis and Betteridge (2024) highlight that not all books are created equal. The Centre for Literacy and Primary Education (CLPE, 2024) confirms the number of representative characters in books are still hugely underrepresented. When children are able to see themselves in books, illustrations and stories this affirms their sense of self and develops belonging and acceptance of oneself.

Connecting with earlier chapters on identity and diversity, the power that stories hold is immense. Families and educators who share these books with children benefit from being knowledgeable of the variety of stories that are published and being able to think critically about the story and whether it will relate to the children they work with. McCormick and McIntosh (2020) explore how stories have transformed literacy in their setting. They share the impact of repeating stories to children with additional needs to be able to develop their enjoyment and connections with the story enabling story retelling and acting.

When children become familiar with stories, they begin to re-enact, or rearrange the story in imaginative ways (Pascal et al., 2026). Here, children might use familiar characters but link their actions to their own experiences to create new stories. When children enact their stories, the power shifts to the child who holds the narrative and direction, enabling their confidence, expression and an affirmation of their views and ideas.

Rabi (aged three), a quiet child, was asked by Charlie the educator if he wanted to share his story. Rabi did so in whispers. 'Plane flying, plane crashed'. He was immensely proud and was willing to act out the story with a small group. He took charge by choosing to pretend to be an aeroplane and act out his story. Charlie sensitively ensured the group he was acting it out to were familiar with Rabi and kept the group quite small to ensure that Rabi was comfortable with expressing himself to his peers. Rabi felt empowered by this process, and became interested in making marks about his story and building aeroplanes using construction materials and recycled materials. When children, like Rabi, are captivated by their play, they may make props, engage in storying, songs or dance to capture a moment of their play. Imray et al. (2023) note that open ended play provides depth and breadth. If Charlie had noticed Rabi's interests and given him a toy aeroplane, this would have limited what he was able to do. Instead, Charlie observed him using recycled boxes and joining them together to create a plane. As he continued, Rabi created more intricate aeroplanes with windows, and propellers. Each time Rabi made this prop it became increasingly elaborate.

In the same way that play enables children's freedom of speech and expression, literacy, including reading and writing can provide an agreed code for representing language.

Wyse and Hacking (2024) argue that in England phonics has become the dominant approach in teaching children how to read and write often forgetting the holistic aspect of reading. They encourage educators to inspire a love of reading and writing through meaningful approaches. This includes teaching phonics as well as using real stories, sharing stories and different motivations for writing to enable children to see how written language can be understood.

When settings work closely with families and the community it can affect children's lives (Joshi, 2024, 2025a, 2025b, 2025c, 2025d; Whalley, 2017). Educators need to consider how they support families in engaging in literacy. One setting established 'Family Fridays' where families would come and read with the children. Some children whose parents were working joined with other family members and would read in a small group. This encouraged families in sharing books at home and ensuring they were utilizing the nursery library as well as local community libraries. Bloch (2024) discusses the connections between language learning and brain development through the Froebelian concept of unity and connectedness. The brain's plasticity enables humans to make the connections through music and language and, as Froebel's writing on the Family (Mother) songs highlights, there is huge importance in singing, particularly lullabies for babies and young children (Powell and Goouch, 2019). These songs are the 'precursor to stories' and can offer 'rich and nourishing learning encounters' (Bloch, 2024: 428). The songs that families sing in the home, like language, passes through generations and can offer a deeper connection to a sense of self and identity. Bloch (2024: 431) adds, 'regular storytelling and story acting help deepen relationships and authentic communication'. Froebelian educators recognize the power of language and expression through storytelling and creativity, building on these forms as modes of communication. Social justice and individual rights are grounded in the concept of expression and freedom of speech. Being able to communicate in whichever method can enable social justice being achieved.

CHAPTER 9

Freedom of Worship: Beliefs, Culture and Nature

This chapter explores how freedom of worship can be reflected on and addressed to ensure that all children are able to live to their fullest, engage with their innermost ideas about their place in the world and be responsible citizens towards others and the natural environment. The themes that arise from the notion of worship are Beliefs, Culture and Nature. Exploration includes how educators might be able to reflect on their practice and enable children and their families be free to hold their personal beliefs, cultures and know how to respect nature.

Freedom of worship explores the idea of 'worth ship' as Gregory in Bruce (1987) describes. This means the coming together of individuals to look at worthwhile ideas for a better world. Social justice includes the right for individuals and communities to engage in nature, songs, celebrations and culture. And finding ways to express beliefs, religion and spirituality in educational and childhood contexts. These ideas may not always be tangible but are felt through connection with others and the wider world. They encompass feelings of belonging, identity, diversity and self-esteem. These concepts can be quite private and may not be shared explicitly, however implicitly, this may be apparent through values and beliefs that are held by individuals in the way they act, work or interact with others. There is an intersection of worship which includes secular and religious aspects of traditions, culture and rituals. These are intertwined and sometimes individuals are unsure if reasons behind the particular aspect can be defined as religious, cultural or a familial tradition.

The United Nations Convention of the Rights of the Child (UNCRC) specifically states that the purpose of education should support children's development to their fullest sense of being with respect for the natural environment, cultural identity, language and values. This includes children's understanding of peoples from different ethnic, national and religious groups (UNICEF, 1989). How this is implemented in educational contexts can be seen through daily routines, policies, curricula and community-based work within and around the setting.

In Froebel's context, Christianity was predominant; however, it can be inferred from his writing that he was hugely influenced by Romanticism and the Enlightenment period. This time in history is connected with self-consciousness, science and nature (Lilley, 1967). The ideas of Romanticism and Enlightenment may have stemmed from indigenous thinking which was prevalent through Asian countries, where movement from Prussia and German states to India and China were recorded (Manjapra, 2014). Education that connects mind, body and spirit is what Froebel had intended. These concepts chime with many indigenous practices which hold deep ideas about the connection of the inner worlds of self to the outer worlds with some practices using the term 'soul' instead of spirit.

Religious worship, practice and beliefs

Children and families may have an interdependent connection between culture and spiritual or religious beliefs. As children live and belong in these spaces, these are infused into educational settings as they become confident in expressing their identity and home life. When Krish (aged five) started attending a Christian school he noticed that all the children said a prayer before eating. Krish wasn't quite sure what this meant and how to or whether or not to participate, so went home and asked his parents. They explained in a way that made connections to their own home cultures and beliefs. 'It's just like how we offer our Gods a small meal to say thank you before we eat.' Krish understood immediately and was able to connect his practices with the ones that were happening at school. Young children will be very aware of their families' religious practices as well as attitudes towards other religious groups. They may begin to have their own ideas or questions about God and concepts around creation, life and death. Educators need to be confident in engaging in discussions with children who are exploring these ideas as well as ensuring that negative attitudes are not adopted as this is an important aspect of ensuring discriminatory views and prejudice are ended (Derman-Sparks et al., 2020; Pemberton, 2025).

Polly observed Adan (aged three) and Noah (aged three) in the nursery. Adan was kneeling and Noah was imitating. Polly asked what they were doing. 'I'm teaching Noah how to pray' Adan explained. This observation showed how confident Adan felt bringing a part of his religious culture and identity to the setting sharing and explaining this with his friend. Noah also respected Adan and his different religious practices and was willing to learn about his friend's life. This interaction demonstrated the safe space that was created in the setting with Adan's culture, religion and ritual being respected and celebrated. Organizations such as The Inter Faith Network (2025) and Humanists UK (2025) promote conversation with others about their faith and beliefs, enabling a sense of respect with deeper understanding of similarity and difference. Humanism and collectivist cultures promote an ethical economic society which is in opposition to competitive, individualistic attitudes. This decolonial frame aligns with many traditional African societies which existed prior to colonialism. Following the shifts in African countries where colonialism was rejected, the humanistic and collective nature of African traditions were promoted. However the ingrained nature of colonial behaviour led to political fragmentation so these frameworks were never fully realized (Murove, 2020). Humanism offers a way of being that counters many colonial perspectives. Froebelian concepts align closely with Humanism and Freire's (1998) ideas of critical consciousness which include supporting children's questioning and critical thinking. Kumru (2025) explores Philosophy for Children (P4C) which supports their thinking about conceptual topics and brings to light their ideas and ways for enacting this in their spaces.

'We think it is important that everyone, whether they are religious or non-believers, should think about the big questions and should never just accept what they are told. This doesn't mean you can't continue to have a religious belief, but if you do you will know that it's your own, not just an unthinking acceptance of someone else's ideas' (Rosen and Young, 2015: 4).

Karina, an educator, wore a hijab every day. The children who were used to seeing her with her hijab assumed that there was no hair under her scarf so considered the hijab material as hair. When some of her hair was poking out, Karina started to fix her hijab. The children then began to ask questions about her hair. Karina had a relationship with all the children and their families. She knew how to give them information that would satisfy their curiosity and provide an opportunity to understand someone close to them but different. Karina explored this further with the children who were interested, and offered stories with illustrations of children with head coverings. She shared pictures of lots of different children and adults wearing hijabs to show the variety of people that want to represent their religion in this way. She made links to children's own West African culture by sharing pictures of head wraps that are worn during celebrations. All these opportunities embedded a deeper understanding and respect for those who covered their hair in a way which was connected with children's own experiences. When Froebel writes about his ideas for education, he includes the spiritual development of children. He highlights the need for authentic and meaningful connections between self and others, extending to larger more abstract concepts of the universe and divinity (Tang and Zhao, 2024).

Often a country's calendar dictates the dominance of certain religions. For example, in the UK, the school and public holidays are centred around celebrations such as Easter and Christmas. Whereas not all families will celebrate these holidays and instead will take off days to celebrate their own festivals. Increasingly in the UK efforts are being made in early childhood settings and schools to consider inclusivity by offering additional days for Eid, Diwali, Vaisakhi, Pongal and Hannukah particularly in areas of higher diverse religious beliefs. Taking into account how children and families may be celebrating these festivals can be included into the seasonal calendar and curriculum to embed an appreciation of the myriads of festivals that are being celebrated. Referring back to Chapter 5, where Radhi and Rakesh were chastised for celebrating a religious festival, there are more settings promoting inclusivity of religion and trying to bring together the home life with opportunities for sharing and discussion.

Scanning the horizon of global perspectives of religion deduced from media and dominant narratives, highlights those which have a superior position in the hierarchies of difference. These may be certain religions which have political and socio-economic alignment with dominant cultures of that country. For example, Christianity and most European countries have a closer connection due to the historical links to the Roman Empire and later connections to the Enlightenment period (Sullivan, 2001). Although it is important to note that the Abrahamic religions (Christianity, Islam and Judaism) started from similar roots and later branched off all within the vicinity of Southwest Asia and Northern Africa. In some nations, the culture is centred around Islamic calendars. This then leads to religious practices which are seen as 'outsider' with governments banning or enforcing certain rules around religious attire. For example, in France wearing the hijab for Muslim women in certain institutions such as school and for sports is banned. Whereas on the opposite end of the scale, in Afghanistan and Iran it is a mandatory to wear a hijab (Ahmad et al., 2022). Interconnecting with the chapter on freedom of speech, being free to express one's religion is a personal matter, and often political narratives are absorbed into systems and enforced. These are infused into governmental policies and eventually hearts and minds which can lead to prejudice and discrimination. Cohen and Tufail (2017) argue that the Prevent policy in the UK which reports a higher policing of those who are Muslim, is igniting Islamophobia within educational settings. Reflecting on biases around religion and ensuring that these are countered is an important step in working towards freedom of worship.

Froebel's writing mentions God and spirit throughout. He was a devout Christian. However his writing does not show the language or dogma that is used in what is conventional in Christianity particularly at that time (Bruce, 2021). It seems as though his writing aligns with a more spiritual aspect of God which can be aligned with a panentheistic perspective. Panentheism believes that the divine intersects the universe. Froebel's fluidity of spirituality and religion connects with a multicultural and evolving aspect of society, beliefs and ideas. It also agrees with his educational philosophy which includes Nature and the agency of young children through this lens of spirituality. 'Education is in the feeling and the sensation, as well as in the anticipation, this must necessarily early find it's suitable nourishment, even with the first development of the child's body, limbs, sense and spirit' (Froebel, 1899: 17). His ideas can be used to explore social justice through the themes of peace woven into his work (Neumann, 2024). Interpreting the concepts of worship without Froebel's ideas of spirituality can lose the wholeness that he intends within his work (Bruce et al., 2024).

Taking part in cultural rituals of shared worth

A more secular form of worship in the context of culture, family traditions and regular rituals can make up an essential element of an individual (Day, 2013). These include celebrations and a sense of awe and wonderment when taking part in something of shared worth. For example, when Nina turned three she took part in a head shaving ritual which is common for those in the Pashtun culture. Within cultures there can be many sects and parts that have different traditions. These cultural aspects can be created from a time and space and then passed on. This then contributes to the culture of that individual, which is learned, borrowed and continues to be adapted over time.

Derman-Sparks et al. (2020) discuss different aspects of culture that can sometimes be seen or not seen. They describe this as deep or surface culture. Being able to recognize children and their families deep culture enables an affirmation and acknowledgement of experiences and identities. It can influence how a family raises their children. There can be some fixed aspects that cultures uphold, but individuals may feel that these are outdated and need evolving. This can cause disruption and disconnection when there are opposing views.

Educators might see children's culture in their settings through their rituals or behaviours. When Efraim (aged three) started the nursery, whenever he came onto the carpet, he would take his shoes off. The educators were unsure why, but when Nian a South East Asian educator came to the setting, she explained that it was often a cultural practice in many Asian households. Her offering of cultural knowledge enabled the rest of the team to understand Efraim's behaviour. Hyland (2010) highlights the need for educators to have culturally relevant knowledge is vital in ensuring that behaviours are understood and respected and to embody a social justice perspective through educational practice.

Sometimes cultures inform a setting's systems and structures. For example, one setting had proudly organized all their resources. In their store cupboard were resources for all different cultures and festivals. When it was Lunar New Year, they brought down the box with all the resources and decorated the classroom for a week. After it was over, it was returned to the box and stored away for the following year. The same was done for other celebrations such as Easter, Mother's Day, Halloween and Diwali. It is important to get this right as there is a fine line between cultural appropriation and cultural *appreciation* (Derman-Sparks et al., 2020). Often, there is a focus on the external aspects of culture – food, holidays, clothing and artefacts, however there are many internal and deep parts of culture that are harder to explain and not always shared by all – values, religion, work, language, relationships.

The setting did not realize the touristic approach it was taking towards these celebrations (Derman-Sparks et al., 2020). They offered a superficial celebration which barely explored the rituals, songs or cultures within each of the festivals. What the setting needed to realize was that the reality of celebrating these festivals didn't happen in a week; instead, this took months of preparing, busyness within the home and visits to family members, shopping trips, new clothes and lots of cleaning. These rituals are just one aspect of celebrating a festival, with each family celebrating special days in their own unique ways. When children are able to step into a world which is different to theirs and make links and connections to their own experiences, the respect for the culture they are experiencing will deepen.

Songs and worship

One way in which culture influences is through the songs that are sung at home or in places of worship – in both secular and religious spaces, and repeated in the setting. Jabari (aged four) was excited when the class was singing 'Yellow Bird' a Haitian creole song that was familiar to him. 'My Mum used to sing that to me as a baby!' Jabari's excitement and sense of identity was affirmed in that experience, highlighting how songs can have a profound impact on children and families. Heritage, language, worship and culture are passed on through songs and hold important value and emotion that can impact all who are involved in a holistic way. Powell and Goouch (2019) show that when singing in groups, the individual heartbeats are synchronized and there is a sense of collective release and somatic freedom in a bodily and spiritual sense improving well-being. There is a connection between those who are singing that is transcendental between time and space.

Lullabies that are sung to babies before birth and after birth show the link between intra-action and deep connection (Barad, 2010). Debbie who worked in the hospital was speaking with a parent whose child was in an incubator. She was showing signs of depression and was worried about connecting with her baby. Debbie suggested that she sing to her baby in the incubator. When the parent tried this, the baby responded and this eased their worries. Lullabies themselves can be soothing not just for baby, but also for the family who sing the song. These all demonstrate the interpersonal relationships that embody concepts such as containment, intersubjectivity which all look at the emotional holding of one another (May and Carr, 2015).

Often songs can bring people together, which is an important aspect of worship both in a secular and religious sense. In one setting, stay and plays with a song time at the end were a regular part of the termly calendar. In these sessions the educators asked families to count down in their own home language whilst singing the song 'Zoom Zoom Zoom, we're going to the moon'. With their child they sang their home languages to them and offered a sense of home. This was one way to bring together the home life to the setting. This invitation was built upon, families who were willing, sang their cultural songs with the group. They were encouraged to sing to their child, instead of just to the group. Educators noticed the eye contact, focus and attention that was held by the child and their family member, they observed a deepening relationship between family and child. The introduction of songs in this way developed the settings repertoire and brought together the community (Barnes, 2019).

Froebel's own work was hugely influenced by what he observed with mothers and their babies. His work on the Family Songs which encompasses all of his ideas in education uses the songs in fivefold development: children's attachment with carer, physical, emotional and moral development as well as linking to the real-world community in Froebel's time (Froebel, 1844). The use of traditional singing is part of the human experience, in South Indian traditions Carnatic music was embedded and ingrained in culture, however as the British Empire continued to colonize India, singers began to adapt the traditions of this type of singing with western classical music creating a modern version and in doing so lost its traditional roots (Mamidipudi and Murthy, 2023). Encouraging families to sing to their children in home languages or with traditional lullabies and songs underpins Froebel's ideas of connecting with the child through song and music whilst developing elements of child development. It also holds the history and traditions of the family at the heart which transcend time and space.

Another way to experience culture is through movement and dance. When Rani went to South Africa she watched the children perform a traditional Zulu dance which was passed onto the children from their families. Traditional dancing told stories of their history, beliefs and culture. Their movements were large, with high kicks, slamming feet down which required a huge amount of balance and coordination. In a more recent time in South Africa a newer dance was formed during apartheid which was created by those working in the mines and wearing 'gum boots'. The dance is named after these boots, which was recreated for Rani when she visited a setting for older children. In synchronized movements the children slapped their boots and body to create rhythm and beat. The dance told a painful story through its rhythm of the longing for freedom. The gumboot dance is specifically taught to children to pass on the history and storytelling of a space and time in South Africa's history. In Palestine, social media posts show children dancing traditional Palestinian dances holding onto their heritage, of which its existence is threatened. These posts share the surrounding destruction of their homes. These dances bring people together in times of deep tragedy and distress. These same social justice issues pervade through these forms of movement representing social injustice and storytelling.

When Froebelians visit countries such as Australia, New Zealand, Japan and South Africa it is extremely important to reflect on what they bring to the native traditions and heritages of that country without imposing European settler contexts (Cooper and Rockel, 2024; Matsumura, 2024). Being aware of the tensions, where it is appropriate to introduce Froebel, or if at all, and where to utilize cultural practices to enable educators to deeply connect with the cultures of the children and community (Bloch and Moodley, 2026). When Rani visited South Africa, she noticed the dances she saw were creative, told deep stories and strongly held traditions. However, the educators she worked with in the early childhood setting shared literal ideas when creating puppets. For example, creating Goldilocks with gold material, writing in books with sentences which literally describe their creations 'this is my house'. Rani's reflection questioned whether this was a generational impact of colonialism in tempering with the ability to think freely and creatively when in an educational context. Jilani (2024) explores Fanon's work who looks at creativity as a decolonial act, which enables an opening up and imagining of new possibilities.

Connecting nature and 'worth-ship'

There are some trendy ways of living which have roots to indigenous practices. Examples of this in today's society include yoga, meditation, acupuncture, wellness practices and ayurvedic traditions and remedies. Often these practices are closely linked to nature and inner mind-body-soul connections. Those looking to colonize these practices remove any link to the original, by renaming and losing the tradition or reasoning behind this. For example, in some early childhood settings, yoga is taught to children, but often without any mention or discussion of where these movements and practices come from (Wolff and Stapp, 2019). Yoga itself means 'union'; it isn't an exercise but instead a deep religious and spiritual connection between the body and soul. These traditions and positions are inspired by nature, with the body reflecting the moon, dogs, cows, sticks, trees and so on. The language in yoga is from Sanskrit, a classical language that originates from around first century BC (Cardona and Luraghi, 2018). The sacred and deeply spiritual practice forms much of Indo-Aryan philosophy which is translated into many Hindu practices today. In these settings, yoga is used as an exercise or for mindfulness to calm disruptive behaviour (Wilkin et al., 2025; Wolff and Stapp, 2019). Whilst there are useful practical applications for yoga in a setting, the history and intentionality of the practice is completely ignored. Froebel's own writing on the Mother (Family) songs are so closely linked to nature and the community, including physical development and connecting with oneself. With extracts from his writing which could be inferred through a spiritual, health and well-being lens, it is possible that Froebel's deep connection with nature is of its own formation however his positionality can be seen as complicit in colonial perspectives through the time and place he is situated in (Froebel, 1844; Joshi, 2019).

With an increasing emphasis on the care and conservation of nature, a form of colonialism named 'green colonialism' is applied to those living in indigenous territories and communities. These build upon the historic actions of colonialism (Islam et al., 2024). Governments and businesses closely monitor the economic benefits of placing renewable and sustainable energy practices within these indigenous areas, but 'tune out' the people's concerns, needs and experiences (Ramirez et al., 2024). The focus on the 'green' environmental factors masks the colonialism taking place. Those in these powerful positions use and abuse nature which fragments, dismantles and destroys indigenous ways of living. This includes traditional practices which respect and know about nature, being in nature and working with it rather than controlling it. Freedom of worship looks to reconnect with nature in ways that prioritizes meaning and authenticity towards the human-nature relationship.

There is an increasing emphasis in early childhood education and care towards the importance and value in engaging with nature. It is driven by the human impact of irreversible environmental damage. There is a narrative which suggests that children will bear the consequences and responsibility to reduce the damage. Environmental education holds stewardship in high regard, and places a high importance on children as these stewards. Shifting these paradigms to a being *in* and learning *with* instead of 'about' offers alternative and more connected pedagogy and recognizes the entanglement of children with nature and respecting their agency in the environment (Taylor, 2013).

Educators need to be thoughtful in how they support children's own engagement with nature (d'Ascoli and Hunter, 2022; Tovey, 2022). Anji and Peter (aged two) went for a walk in a local park and came across a bridge with water moving in a steady flow. Anji offered a leaf from the ground to place in the water and watch the leaf flow to the other side (see Figure 9.1). With Peter's interest piqued, he found more leaves to add to this for his own experimentation. Engaging in nature can be so powerful. It can enable exploration of the concepts of water flow, movement and physics through simple observations and actions. Peter and Anji were free to explore nature, it's awe and wonderment and come together with their own ideas about the environment around them. Much of Froebelian practice supports engagement with nature, holding nature as its first teacher. However, Howe (2022) notes that nature alone does not automatically transfer knowledge to those within it, instead it is the role of a knowledgeable educator who can bring out this learning for children.

Nature in the community relies upon the access and knowledge of being able to engage in the natural world. Louv (2008) discusses what he calls a 'nature deficit disorder'. He argues that this condition is prevalent in childhood which has

FIGURE 9.1 Peter by the water.

an unhealthy attachment to electronic devices. However, much of his work fails to discuss the access requirements needed to be able to engage in nature to address these attachments (Early Education and Froebel Trust, 2022). An increase in the provision of outdoor only nurseries is becoming popular in typically wealthier areas within the UK. This demonstrates the widening gap between those who can access nature opposed to those who cannot. This is then left to educators to imagine and creatively bring in nature to settings where heavily concreted gardens form their outdoor space. Systems within settings which enable free flow play from indoor to outdoor provide children with access to nature. Supporting research shows that those who spend time in nature are more likely to respect it, compared with those who don't and begin to fear nature (Tovey, 2007). Razzall (2024) adds how individuals learn together, forming community through engaging in nature and providing a genuine form of awe and wonderment. Froebel described this process as the ultimate teacher.

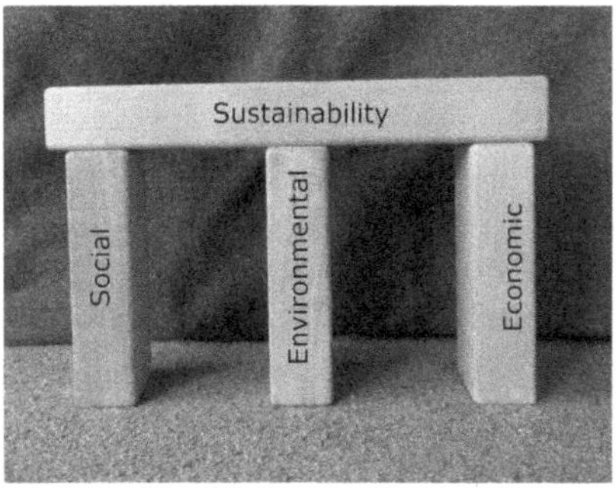

FIGURE 9.2 The three pillars of sustainability.

A wider acknowledgement of the crisis in nature depletion has demanded the formation of the United Nations Sustainable Development Goals (United Nations, 2015). Using these goals alongside the three pillars of sustainability enable a social, environmental and economic evaluation of sustainability in learning contexts – see Figure 9.2 (Purvis et al., 2019). Highlighting the interconnection of education, health, nature and sustainability through goals which are applicable in governmental targets, they show the importance of each member of humanity contributing towards sustainability. This is supported by Taylor (2013) who highlights the responsibility must not fall on children, indigenous groups or communities.

Yet, a colonial legacy which has impacted nature and the environment cannot be ignored. A common settler mindset was to plant trees on the land where they settle. This has a huge impact on the plants and forests generations later. Raging wildfires in Palestine and South Africa for example are the result of European settler planting of European pine whose non-native roots draw huge amounts of water leading to drought, food scarcity and readily flammable bush (Nazzal, 2019; Wolfe, 2006).

Understanding where materials come from and what is native or non-native to the earth in particular regions creates questions of where the materials such as cotton may have come from and the impact of trade movement through the British empire. This highlights the interweaving of settler and indigenous practices and an acknowledgement of colonialism, slavery and the generational impact of this which survives through nature. In Australian and New Zealand contexts engaging with nature often stems from indigenous practices but it is woven into contemporary practice through the entanglement of pedagogy. New Zealand's Te whariki curriculum is an exemplary model in the weaving of native heritage and current contexts (Nuttall, 2013). Knowing where materials come from is an important aspect of Froebelian education. In Froebel's school in Keilhau, Nauer (2023) explains how children are encouraged to question how the chairs they sit on are made. They backtrack the steps from carpentry to forestry and are urged to respect the process in which their materials are made (Moorhouse, 2021). Through this a respect of nature is implemented. Tovey (2007) highlights the importance of enabling children's play outdoors and the result of this supports their love for and caring for nature. Asking children to care for something they have not fully experienced themselves aligns with Taylor's (2013) writing on asking children to be responsible for saving the earth without having a deep connection to it. The Te Whariki curriculum framework embodies much of Froebelian philosophy through the influence of Helen May (May and Carr, 2015).

This begs the question of whether Froebelian philosophy and principles are of a European settler context or provide an interweaving of pedagogy and indigenous practices to an educational perspective. Perhaps this is based on the intention of the Froebelian who is invited into these spaces and the way in which they are able to observe, reflect on and offer a connecting perspective to explore these educational practices. Or perhaps by the disposition of a Froebelian, the approach would always look to start from what the context is and guide pedagogy from here, whilst maintaining the connection to nature, spirituality and worth-ship.

CHAPTER 10

Participation

This book has examined the themes and freedoms relating to social justice. It has addressed issues relating to Identity (Chapter 2), Diversity (Chapter 3), Equality (Chapter 4) and Equity (Chapter 5) threaded through a Froebelian perspective with examples of how they relate to implementation in practice.

Young (2024: 39) writes, 'those with lived experience should be at the centre of policies intended to improve their circumstances, and have a platform from which to speak themselves'. This is the essence of access, action and participation. Being motivated by personal matters and having opportunities and access to express these views is the bedrock of democracy (Bello-Bravo et al., 2022). Abdallah (2025) explains how participation is motivated by the feeling of being needed and mattering – all linking to the connection with others, finding similarities and affirming identities through these relationships.

Froebelian principles and social justice

The Froebelian principles and philosophy have been threaded throughout this book to affirm the ability to maintain a philosophical framework whilst working towards social justice. The Froebel Trust's (2021) eight principles each promote this worldview.

Unity and connectedness highlight this interconnected approach. Building on these connections enables the appreciation and celebration of individuals and communities within society. By understanding that children's experiences are connected in a holistic way can support educators in facilitating these links to their identity and diversity.

Children as *autonomous learners* provide the foreground to trust children's intentions, respecting who they are and what they want and need. A participatory environment and collective community enable children's agency of their own learning.

Valuing childhood in its own right directly connects with the United Nations Convention on the Rights of the Child (UNCRC). These are a foundational aspect to the inclusion of children within society that is fair and equitable.

Relationships matter includes the connection with family members, peers, community and spirituality, culture, religion and nature. It highlights the relationship with oneself – developing self-awareness, critical consciousness and the ability to reflect and take action to address issues.

Creativity and the power of symbols promote expression and speech; this principle supports children's individuality and diversity and form a path to participation (Beljan, 2025).

The central importance of play ties in with children's rights to play, the expression of inner worlds and experimenting with new experiences. Educators who embody this principle well, know to find the balance between freedom and guidance and utilize the twelve features of play (Bruce, 1987, 1991, 2021).

Engaging with nature supports children's ability to find their place within a wider world, being able to care for another living thing is later afforded to themselves and the relationships they cultivate. It includes the spiritual aspect of awe and wonderment and how to consciously learn with the natural world alongside indigenous people and practices.

Knowledgeable, nurturing educators embody these principles and find they are constantly on the path to developing their own professional learning through reflection on how they impact the children, families and communities they work with.

Froebelian principles are an essential part of social justice. They form a philosophical core a multitude of frameworks lean on. These include the Universal Declaration of Human Rights (UDHR), the UNCRC, Sustainable Development Goals, three pillars of sustainability and the four freedoms: from fear, want, of speech and worship. Social justice cannot be formed in silos; it depends on participation by each and every individual playing their part in developing a fair and equitable world for ourselves and the future generations to come.

REFERENCES

Abdallah, M. (2025) 'To Belong Is Not Enough'. Available at: https://mabdallah.substack.com/p/to-belong-is-not-enough 2025. (Accessed: 1 June 2025).

Abrams, F. (2019) 'Equality in Schools: "What Makes People Think a Black Woman Can't Be Headteacher?"', *The Guardian*. Available at: https://www.theguardian.com/education/2019/oct/22/equality-schools-what-makes-people-think-black-woman-cant-be-headteacher. (Accessed: 26 May 2025).

Adams, H., and E. Short (2025) *Creating Environments for Children to Play and Learn*. Online: Froebel Trust.

Adichie, C. N. (2009) *The Danger of a Single Story*. YouTube: TED.

Adonis, C. K., and F. Silinda (2021) 'Institutional Culture and Transformation in Higher Education in Post-1994 South Africa: A Critical Race Theory Analysis', *Critical African Studies*, 13(1): 73–94.

Adshead, G. (2024) 'Is Violence Normal?' *Reith Lectures*. London: BBC Radio 4.

Ahmad, N., H. H. B. D. H. A. Aziz and S. N. B. Edirahman (2022) 'Religious Freedom and the Hijab Controversy: A Human Rights Perspective', *Manchester Journal of Transnational Islamic Law and Practice*, 18(1), pp. 30–51.

Al Jazeera (2024) 'Which Countries Recognise Palestine in 2024?'. Al Jazeera. Available at: https://www.aljazeera.com/news/2024/11/29/which-countries-recognise-palestine-in-2024. (Accessed: 9 February 2025).

Amnesty International (2025) 'Freedom of Expression'. Available at: https://www.amnesty.org/en/what-we-do/freedom-of-expression/ (Accessed: 3 May 2025).

Archer, N. (2021) 'Agency and Values in Shaping Education Professional Identities', *Early Education Journal*, 95: 4–6.

Athey, C. (1990) *Extending Thought in Young Children*. 1st edn. London: Paul Chapman.

Austin, A., S. L. Craig, S. D'Souza and L. B. McInroy (2022) 'Suicidality Among Transgender Youth: Elucidating the Role of Interpersonal Risk Factors', *Journal of Interpersonal Violence*, 37(5–6), pp. 2696–718.

Barad, K. (2010) 'Quantum Entanglements and Hauntological Relations of Inheritance: Dis/continuities, SpaceTime Enfoldings, and Justice-to-Come', *Derrida Today*, 3(2), pp. 240–68.

Barnes, J. (2019) *The Lullaby Project Five Years On: Evaluating the Well-Being Impact and Legacy of Singing a Child's Story*, Canterbury Christ Church University: Canterbury Christ Church University.

Bartholomew, L., and T. Bruce (1993) *Getting to Know You: Guide to Record-Keeping in Early Childhood Education and Care*. 0–8 Years: The First Phase of Living. London: Hodder Education.

Bateson, S., and S. Tembo (2024) *Playing with Power*. Online: Froebel Trust.

Belbase, S., B. C. Luitel and P. C. Taylor (2008) 'Autoethnography: A Method of Research and Teaching for Transformative Education', *Journal of Education and Research*, 1(1), pp. 86–95.

Beljan, D. J. (2025) 'Pedagogical Understanding: Childhood as a Sphere of Expressivity and Resonance'. *International Froebel Society Conference 2025*, Erfurt, Germany. University of Auckland/NZ.

Bello-Bravo, J., J. W. Medendorp and B. Pittendrigh (2022) 'Just Participation or Just Participation? A Participatory Justice Model for More Successful Theory of Change Design, Implementation, and Solution Uptake', *Heliyon*, 8(7): 1–8.

Bloch, C. (2024) 'Integrative Neuroscience and Froebelian Understandings in Early Childhood Education', in T. Bruce, Y. Nishida, S. Powell, H. Wasmuth and J. Whinnett, (eds.) *The Bloomsbury Handbook to Friedrich Froebel*. London: Bloomsbury, pp. 427–35.

Bloch, C., and G. Ellis (2021) 'Neuroscience and Literacy: An Integrative View', *Transactions of the Royal Society of South Africa*, 76(2): 1–61.

Bloch, C., and T. Moodley (forthcoming) 'Meaningful Early Childhood Education in South Africa: African Indigenous

Educational Understandings and Froebelian Principles', in T. Moodley, S. Stofile and R. Govender (eds) *The Promotion of Holistic and Inclusive Early Childhood Education Practices in South Africa*: AOSIS.

Blythe, S. G. (2017) *Attention, Balance and Coordination: The ABC of Learning Success*. West Sussex: John Wiley & Sons.

Bourke, B. (2014) 'Positionality: Reflecting on the Research Process', *The Qualitative Report*, 19(33), pp. 1–9.

Boussemart, J. P., H. Leleu, Z. Shen and V. Valdmanis (2020) 'Performance Analysis for Three Pillars of Sustainability', *Journal of Productivity Analysis*, 53(3): 305–20.

Bowlby, J. (1979) 'The Bowlby-Ainsworth Attachment Theory', *Behavioral and Brain Sciences*, 2(4), pp. 637–38.

Bragg, S., and J. Ringrose (2023) 'Intervening in School Uniform Debates: Making Equity Matter in England', in R. Shanks, J. Ovington, B. Cross and A. Carnarvon (eds) *School Uniforms. The Cultural and Social Foundations of Education*. London: Palgrave Macmillan, pp. 49–65.

Brent Council (2024) 'Brent Early Years Conference 2024 – Start for Life – Together'. Brent.

Brians, P. P. (2017) *Reason, Romanticism & Revolution*: Washington State University. Available at: https://brians.wsu.edu/2017/04/18/reason-romanticism-revolution/ (Accessed: 25 February 2025).

Brodie, J. (2007) 'Reforming Social Justice in Neoliberal Times', *Studies in Social Justice*, 1(2), pp. 93–107.

Bronfenbrenner, U. (1986) 'Ecology of the Family as Context for Human Development: Research Perspectives', *American Psychological Association*, 22(6), pp. 723–42.

Brookes, L., and J. Frankham (2021) 'The Hidden Voices of Children and Young People with a Parent in Prison: What Schools Need to Know about Supporting These Vulnerable Pupils', *International Journal of Educational Development*, 81.

Bruce, T. (1987) *Early Childhood Education*. London: Hodder and Stoughton.

Bruce, T. (1991) *Time to Play in Early Childhood Education*. Hodder & Stoughton.

Bruce, T. (1996) *Helping Young Children to Play*. London: Hodder and Stoughton.

Bruce, T. (2004) *Cultivating Creativity*. 1st edn. London: Hodder Education.

Bruce, T. (2012) *Early Childhood Practice: Froebel Today*. London: Sage.

Bruce, T. (2015) *Early Childhood Education*. 5th edn. London: Hodder and Stoughton.

Bruce, T. (2019) 'The International Froebel Society', in T. Bruce, P. Elfer, S. Powell and L. Werth (eds) *The Routledge International Handbook of Froebel and Early Childhood Practice*. Oxon: Routledge.

Bruce, T. (2021) *Friedrich Froebel: A Critical Introduction to Key Themes and Debates*. London: Bloomsbury.

Bruce, T. (2023) 'Freedom with Guidance: A Froebelian Approach to Play'. *International Froebel Society Conference 2023*, Ireland: University of Maynooth.

Bruce, T., K. Brehony, L. Werth and S. F. Quinn (2019) 'The Froebel Educational Institute', in T. Bruce, P. Elfer, S. Powell and L. Werth (eds) *The Routledge International Handbook of Froebel and Early Childhood Practice*. Oxon: Routledge.

Bruce, T., and M. Hunter (2019) 'The Froebel Networking Tradition and Kitchen Seminars', in T. Bruce, P. Elfer, S. Powell and L. Werth (eds) *The Routledge International Handbook of Froebel and Early Childhood Practice*. Oxon: Routledge.

Bruce, T., Y. Nishida, S. Powell, H. Wasmuth and J. Whinnett (2024) *The Bloomsbury Handbook to Friedrich Froebel*. London: Bloomsbury.

Cardona, G., and S. Luraghi (2018) 'Sanskrit', *The World's Major Languages*. London: Routledge, pp. 380–98.

Carr, S. (2023) 'Minimum Wage', *Wage and Well-being*. New Zealand: Springer, pp. 117–46.

Chamberlin, L. J. (1970) 'Revolution Vs. Evolution in Education', *American Secondary Education*, 1(1), pp. 22–4.

Child Bereavement UK (n.d.) 'Child Bereavement UK, Rebuilding Lives Together'. Available at: https://www.childbereavementuk.org/Listing/Category/about-child-bereavement-uk (Accessed: 1 July 2025).

Children's Play Advisory Service (2020) 'Overhead Ladders (Monkey Bars) Suggestions for Reducing Risk', http://www.childrensplayadvisoryservice.org.uk/index.html. (Accessed: 8 April 2025).

Clark, A. (2023) *Slow Knowledge and the Unhurried Child*. Contesting Early Childhood. London: Routledge.

Clark, K. B., and M. P. Clark (1996) *Racial Identification and Preference in Negro Children*. Indiana: Bobbs-Merrill.
CLPE (2024) 'Reflecting Realities', www.clpe.org.uk: Centre for Literacy in Primary Education. Available at: https://clpe.org.uk/system/files/2024-12/CLPE%20Reflecting%20Reality%202024%20v6%20WEB.pdf. (Accessed: 9 August 2025).
Cohen, B., and W. Tufail (2017) 'Prevent and the Normalization of Islamophobia', in F. Elahi and O. Khan (eds) *Islamophobia: Still a Challenge for Us All*. London: Runnymede Trust, pp. 41–5.
Cooper, D. M. (2025) 'Ka Mua, Ka Muri (Walking Backwards Into the Future): Nurturing the Whole Child Across Time and Place', *International Froebel Society Conference 2025*, Erfurt, Germany: University of Auckland/NZ.
Cooper, M., and J. Rockel (2024) 'Pedagogies of Care with One-Year-Olds: A Contemporary Froebelian Lens in New Zealand', in T. Bruce, Y. Nishida, S. Powell, H. Wasmuth and J. Whinnett (eds) *The Bloomsbury Handbook to Friedrich Froebel*. London: Bloomsbury, p. 288.
Crenshaw, K. (2015) 'Why Intersectionality Can't Wait', *Washington Post*, 24 September 2015.
Crew, T. (2024) 'Disadvantaged, Discriminated Against and Ignored: The Experiences of Romani and Gypsy Travellers', in S. Iafrati and L. Gregory (eds) *Diversity and Welfare Provision*. Bristol: Policy Press, pp. 117–35.
Cushing, I. (2021) '"Say It Like the Queen": The Standard Language Ideology and Language Policy Making in English Primary Schools', *Language, Culture and Curriculum*, 34(3): 321–36.
Cushing, I. (2023) 'Word Rich or Word Poor? Deficit Discourses, Raciolinguistic Ideologies and the Resurgence of the 'Word Gap' in England's Education Policy', *Critical Inquiry in Language Studies*, 20(4): 305–31.
Cushing, I. (2025) 'Social In/Justice and the Deficit Foundations of Oracy', *Oxford Review of Education*, pp. 396–413.
Cushing, I., and J. Snell (2023) 'The (White) Ears of Ofsted: A Raciolinguistic Perspective on the Listening Practices of the Schools Inspectorate', *Language in Society*, 52(3), pp. 363–86.
d'Ascoli, H., and D. Hunter (2022) 'Re-Engaging with Nature'. Online: Froebel Trust.
Davies, M. (2003) *Movement and Dance in Early Childhood*. 0–8 series. 2nd edn. London: Paul Chapman.

Davis, A., Juliet Stone, Chloe Blackwell, Matt Padley, Claire Shepherd and D. Hirsch (2022) *A Minimum Income Standard for the United Kingdom in 2022*, Loughborough University. Available at: https://repository.lboro.ac.uk/articles/report/A_Minimum_Income_Standard_for_the_United_Kingdom_in_2022/21206114/1?file=37603742. (Accessed: 28 July 2025).

Day, C. B. (2013) 'Culture and Identity Development: Getting Infants and Toddlers Off to a Great Start', in E. A. Virmani and P. Mangione (eds) *A Guide to Culturally Sensitve Care*. 2nd ed. California: WestEd, pp. 2–10.

Delgado, R., and J. Stefancic (2023) *Introduction to Critical Race Theory. The Bible and Cultural Studies: Critical Readings*. USA: Bloomsbury Academic.

Denton, A., and D. L. Parker (2024) 'Cooking with Young Children'. Online: Froebel Trust.

Department for Education, Education, D.f. (2014) 'Guidance on promoting British values in schools'. https://www.gov.uk/government/news/guidance-on-promoting-british-values-in-schools-published. (Accessed: 9 March 2025).

Derman-Sparks, L., J. Olsen Edwards and C. M. Goins (2020) *Anti-Bias Education for Young Children & Ourselves*. Washington DC: naeyc.

Diaz, C. J. (2003) 'Latino/a Voices in Australia: Negotiating Bilingual Identity', *Contemporary Issues in Early Childhood*, 4(3), pp. 314–36.

Diverse Educators (2024) 'Our DEI Glossary'. Online: Diverse educators. Available at: https://www.diverseeducators.co.uk/our-dei-glossary/ (Accessed: 1 February 2025).

Diverse Educators (2025) Diverse Educators website. Online: Diverse Educators,. Available at: https://www.diverseeducators.co.uk/ (Accessed: 1 April 2025).

Done, E. J., and M. J. Andrews (2020) 'How Inclusion Became Exclusion: Policy, Teachers and Inclusive Education', *Journal of Education Policy*, 35(4): 447–64.

Done, E. J., H. Knowler and D. Armstrong (2021) '"Grey" Exclusions Matter: Mapping Illegal Exclusionary Practices and the Implications for Children with Disabilities in England and Australia', *Journal of Research in Special Educational Needs*, 21(S1): 36–44.

Downs, W., H.o.C. Library (2024) 'Policing response to the 2024 summer riots': UK Parliament.
Drew, I., R. Pierre, R. Sen and C. Kerr (2023) 'Exploring and Re-Imagining Children's Services in England Through a Decolonial Frame', in S. R and K. C (eds) *The Future of Children's Care: Critical Perspectives on Children's Services Reform*. Bristol: Policy Press, pp. 101–21.
Early Education and Froebel Trust (2022) 'The Access to Nature Project - A Guide for Educators'. Online: Froebel Trust.
Eisenberg, A. (2006) 'Education and the Politics of Difference: Iris Young and the Politics of Education', *Educational Philosophy and Theory*, 38(1): 7–23.
Elfer, P. (2024) *Talking with Feeling in the Early Years*. Oxon: Routledge.
Ellemers, N., R. Spears and B. Doosje (2002) 'Self and Social Identity', *Annual Review of Psychology*, 53: 161–86.
Ellmers, T. J., M. R. Wilson, E. C. Kal and W. R. Young (2022) 'Standing Up To Threats: Translating the Two-System Model of Fear to Balance Control in Older Adults', *Experimental Gerontology*, 158: 1–10.
End Sexism in Schools (2025) 'School Uniform Policies'. Online. Available at: https://endsexisminschools.org.uk/campaign-projects/school-uniform-policy/ (Accessed: 18 April 2025).
FDR library (n.d.) *FDR and the Four Freedoms Speech*. Online. Available at: https://www.fdrlibrary.org/four-freedoms (Accessed: 25 July 2025).
Farah (2024) *In Conversation with Warda Farah, Speech and Language Therapist*, 2024. Directed by Films, S.
Fiske, E. B., and H. F. Ladd (2004) *Elusive Equity: Education Reform in Post-Apartheid South Africa*. Washington DC: Brookings Institution Press.
Flewitt, R., and K. Cowan (2020) 'Guidance for Practitioners on Digitial Documentation'. Online: Froebel Trust.
Francis-Devine, B., H.o.C. Library (2025) 'Poverty in the UK: Statistics'. House of Commons Library.
Francis, T. a. (2021) 'What is Social Justice?' Available at: https://insights.taylorandfrancis.com/social-justice/what-is-social-justice/ (Accessed: 23 December 2024).
Freire, P. (1970) *Pedagogy of the Oppressed*. UK: Penguin Random House.

Freire, P. (1994) *Pedagogy of Hope*. Translated by: R. R. Barr. London: Bloomsbury.
Freire, P. (1998) *Pedagogy of Freedom*. Translated by: P. Clarke. Maryland, USA: Rowman & LittleField.
Froebel, F. (1826) *The Education of Man*. New York: D Appleton.
Froebel, F. (1844) *Mother Songs, Games and Stories*. Translated by: F. Lord and E. Lord. Boston: Lee and Shepard.
Froebel, F. (1861) *Pedagogics of the Kindergarten*. Translated by: J. Jarvis. New York: D. Appleton.
Froebel, F. (1899) *Education By Development*. Translated by: J. Jarvis. New York: D. Appleton.
The Froebel Trust (2013) *Discovered Treasure: The Life and Work of Elinor Goldschmied 1910–2009*. Roehampton, UK: The Froebel Trust.
Froebel Trust (2021) 'Froebelian Principles'. Available at: https://www.froebel.org.uk/uploads/documents/Froebelian-Principles-Poster-A4.pdf. (Accessed: 23 December 2024).
Froebel Trust (2022) *Slow Pedagogy - Making Time for Children's Learning and Development*, 2022. Directed by Froebel Trust. UK.
Froebel Trust (2024) 'Outdoor Learning with Young Children'. Online: Froebel Trust.
Furman, G. (2012) 'Social Justice Leadership as Praxis: Developing Capacities Through Preparation Programs', *Educational Administration Quarterly*, 48(2), pp. 191–229.
Gaza Great Minds Foundation (2025) 'Our Impact on Gaza'. Available at: https://gazagreatminds.org/schools/ (Accessed: 8 April 2025).
Gemayel, S. E. (2024) 'From 'Real Spaces' to 'Other Spaces' in Young Refugee Children's Free-Flow Play', in T. Bruce, Y. Nishida, S. Powell, H. Wasmuth and J. Whinnett (eds) *The Bloomsbury Handbook to Friedrich Froebel*. London: Bloomsbury, pp. 311–18.
Ghosh, R., A. A. Abdi and M. A. Naseem (2008) 'Identity in Colonial and Postcolonial Contexts', in A. A. Abdi and G. Richardson (eds) *Decolonizing Democratic Education Bold Visions in Educational Research*. ebook: Brill, pp. 57–66.
Goddard, C. (2024) 'Reflect and Learn', *Nursery Management Today*. https://nmt-magazine.co.uk/feature/reflect-and-learn/. (Accessed: 1 June 2025).

Goldschmied, E., and S. Jackson (2004) *People Under Three: Young Children in Day Care*. London: Psychology Press.

Goldschmied, E., and D. Selleck (1996) *Communication Between Babies in Their First Year, Film and Booklet*. London: National Children's Bureau.

Gorard, S., W. Chen, Y. Tan, B. See, C. Gazmuri, A. Tereshchenko, F. Demie and N. Siddiqui (2023) 'The Disproportionality of Ethnic Minority Teachers in England: Trends, Patterns, and Problems [Version 2; Peer Review: 3 Approved, 1 Approved with Reservations]', *Routledge Open Research*, 2(13): 1–31.

Green, D. (2024) 'Family Songs at Home', in T. Bruce, Y. Nishida,S. Powell, H. Wasmuth and J. Whinnett (eds) *The Bloomsbury Handbook to Friedrich Froebel*. London: Bloomsbury, pp. 264–71.

Gregory, E., and M. Ruby (2011) 'The 'Insider/Outsider' Dilemma of Ethnography: Working with Young Children and Their Families in Cross-Cultural Contexts', *Journal of Early Childhood Research*, 9(2), pp. 162–74.

Grimaldi, E. (2011) 'Neoliberalism and the Marginalisation of Social Justice: The Making of an Education Policy to Combat Social Exclusion', *International Journal of Inclusive Education*, 16(11): 1131–54.

Grooms, A. A., D. Mahatmya and E. T. Johnson (2021) 'The Retention of Educators of Color Amidst Institutionalized Racism', *Educational Policy*, 35(2): 180–212.

Grower, P., L. M. Ward and S. Rowley (2021) 'Beyond Objectification: Understanding the Correlates and Consequences of Sexualization for Black and White Adolescent Girls', *Journal of Research on Adolescence*, 31(2): 273–81.

Guard, C. (2023) '"It's the Little Bits That You Have Enabled Me to See". Reconceptualising the Voices of Babies Using the Video Interaction Dialogue Model with Early Years Educators', *Early Years*, 43(3): 606–25.

Guard, C. (2024) *Hearing the Voices of Babies in Baby-Educator Interactions in Early Childhood Settings*. PhD, Roehampton, UK: University of Roehampton.

Guard, C. (2025) *Rights and Agency for Babies, Toddlers and Young Children*, Oxford, UK: University of Oxford.

Guimarães, S. (2025) 'Understanding Life Changes in Terms of Possiblities', in F. Tang, S. Guimarães and C. Rubiano (eds) *Young Children's Identities*. London: Routledge, pp. 43–54.
Gura, P. (1996) *Resources for Early Learning: Children, Adults and Stuff*. London: Hodder & Stoughton.
Hall, D. J. (2025) 'Early Childhood Education: A System That Shapes Developmental Inequalities', Available at: LinkedIn.
Hamilton and Showunmi (2023) *Helping Young Children to Think about Race in the Early Years*. Online: Anna Freud Centre.
Harding, S. (2024) 'Reflections on Thuringia', *Froebel Gathering 2024*, Roehampton, UK.
Hill, F. (2022) Freedom from Fear. *Reith Lectures*. London: BBC Radio 4.
Holland, P. (2003) *We Don't Play With Guns Here*. Debating Play. Maidenhead: Open University Press.
Holmes, S. (2025) *Re-visiting Home Visits*. Online: Tapestry.
Honneth, A. (2014) *The I in We: Studies in the Theory of Recognition*. John Wiley & Sons.
hooks, b. (1994) *Teaching to Transgress*. New York: Routledge.
hooks, b. (2001) *All About Love*. New York: Harper Collins.
Howe, S. (2022) '(Re)Connecting Pedagogies: Examining the Links between Froebelian and Common Worlds Approaches to Environmental Learning', *Global Education Review*, 9(2), pp. 38–50.
Humanists UK (2025) 'Humanism'. Online. Available at: https://humanists.uk/humanism/ (Accessed: 1 July 2025).
Hyder, T. (2005) *War, Conflict and Play*. Debating Play. Open University Press: Maidenhead.
Hyland, N. E. (2010) 'Social Justice in Early Childhood Classrooms', *Young Children*, 65, pp. 82–7.
Imray, S., T. Thomson and J. Whinnett (2023) *Sewing with Young Children*. Online: Froebel Trust.
The Inter Faith Network (2025) 'Mission Vision and Values'. Online. Available at: https://www.interfaith.org.uk/about/mission-vision-and-values (Accessed: 12 July 2025).
Iser, M. (2019) 'Recognition', The Stanford Encyclopedia of Philosophy. Available at: https://plato.stanford.edu/archives/sum2019/entries/recognition/ (Accessed: 1 February 2025).

Islam, F. B., L. Naylor, J. E. Bryan and D. J. Coker (2024) 'Climate Coloniality and Settler Colonialism: Adaptation and Indigenous Futurities', *Political Geography*, 114, 103164.

James, Z. (2021) 'Roma, Gypsies, and Travellers as a Community of Difference: Challenging Inclusivity as an Anti-racist Approach', *Critical Romani Studies*, 4(2): 142–62.

Jaquiline, A., and F. Daniel Sidney (2025) 'Balancing Child-Centred and Teacher-Centred Didactic Approaches in Early Years Learning', *Education 3–13*, 53(3): 353–65.

Jawad, G. (2020) 'Teaching Identity Formation Through Classroom Practices in the Post-Method Era: A Systematic Review', *Cognet Education*, 7(1), pp. 1–19.

Jena, U. o. (2020) *Famous University Teachers and Students from the History of the University of Jena (Selection)*. Available at: https://www.uni-jena.de/en/109868/famous-university-teachers-and-students-from-the-history-of-the-university-of-jena-selection#head-wrapper (Accessed: 1 July 2025).

Jilani, S. (2024) 'Becoming in a Colonial World: Approaching Subjectivity with Fanon', *Textual Practice*, 38(10): 1583–600.

Joshi, R. 2019. 'Health and Well-Being Froebel and McMillan Perspectives'. Online: ECSDN.

Joshi, R. (2023a) 'The Christmas Show - Is It Still Relevant?'. Available at: https://content.govdelivery.com/accounts/UKISLINGTON/bulletins/3674136. (Accessed: 13 July 2025).

Joshi, R. 2023b. 'Exploring Children's Identity: A Froebelian Perspective'. Online: Froebel Trust Travelling Tutors endorsement presentations.

Joshi, R. (2023c) 'Space'. Available at: https://thefroebelpartnership.co.uk/news/ 2025. (Accessed: 13 March 2025).

Joshi, R. (2024) 'Inclusion, Family and Community'. Available at: https://thefroebelpartnership.co.uk/news/ 2025. (Accessed: 29 July 2025).

Joshi, R. (2025a) 'Advocating for Children and Empowering Families'. https://www.familiesfirstguildford.com/2025/05/02/advocating-for-children-and-empowering-families/. (Accessed: 9 August 2025).

Joshi, R. (2025b) 'Developing Networks and Building community'. https://www.familiesfirstguildford.com/2025/01/24/developing-networks-and-building-community/. (Accessed: 9 August 2025).

Joshi, R. (2025c) 'Journeys with Guildford Family Centre'. https://www.familiesfirstguildford.com/2025/06/23/journeys-with-guildford-family-centre/. (Accessed: 9 August 2025).
Joshi, R. (2025d) 'Keeping the Child at the Centre'. https://www.familiesfirstguildford.com/2024/10/07/keeping-the-child-at-the-centre/. (Accessed: 9 August 2025).
Jost, J. T., and A. C. Kay (2010) 'Social Justice: History, Theory, and Research', in S. T. Fiske, D. T. Gilbert and G. Lindzey (eds) *Handbook of Social Psychology*. 5th edn: John Wiley & Sons Inc, pp. 1122–65.
Kalalo, R. T. (2024) 'The Role and Function of Single Parents in Special Needs Children to Combat Loneliness', *Surabaya Psychiatry Journal/Jurnal Psikiatri Surabaya*, 13(S1): 119–24.
Katz, P. A. and J. A. Kofkin (1997) 'Race, Gender and Young Children', in S. S. Luthar, J. A. Burack, D. Cicchetti and J. R. Weisz (eds) *Developmental Psychopathology: Perspectives on Adjustment, Risk, and Disorder*. Cambridge University Press, pp. 51–74.
Keane, E. (2024) 'Finding Moral Value through Maintaining a Working Class 'Mentality': Student Teachers from Working Class Backgrounds (Not) Becoming Middle Class', *Sociology*, 58(2): 454–70.
Keegan, C. (2024) *"It's Like a Baby Jail!" The Impact of Regimented Daily Routines on Children's Participation in Early Childhood Education*. Doctor of Philosophy in Education, Maynooth University.
Kelly, D., P. Quinn, A. Slater, K. Lee, A. Gibson, M. Smith, L. Ge and O. Pascalis (2005) 'Three-Month-Olds, But Not Newborns, Prefer Own-Race Faces', *Dev Sci*, 8(6), pp. 31–6.
Kent, G. (2005) *Freedom from Want: The Human Right to Adequate Food*. World: Georgetown University Press.
Kethineni, S., M. Srinivasan and S. Kakar (2016) 'Combating Violence against Women in India: Nari Adalats and Gender-Based Justice', *Women & Criminal Justice*, 26(4), pp. 281–300.
Knight, R. (2024) 'Oracy and Cultural Capital: The Transformative Potential of Spoken Language', *Literacy*, 58(1): 37–47.
Konayashi, A. and B. Ray (2000) 'Civil Risk and Landscapes of Marginality in Canada: A Pluralist Approach to Social Justice', *Canadian Geographer / Le Géographe canadien*, 44(4): 401–17.

Kumru, D. B. (2025) 'The Ownership of Wisdom: Provocations on Early Years as a Context for "Thinking Together"'. International Froebel Society Conference 2025.

Laevers, F., and B. Declercq (2018) 'How Well-Being and Involvement Fit Into the Commitment to Children's Rights', *European Journal of Education*, 53(3): 325–35.

Laevers, F., and J. Moons (2008) 'Ten Ways to Enhance Well Being and Involvement: An Introduction in the Ten Action Points'. Centre for experiental education.

Lampert, J., B. Burnett and S. Lebhers (2016) '"More Like the Kids Than the Other Teachers": One Working-Class Pre-Service Teacher's Experiences in a Middle-Class Profession', *Teaching and Teacher Education*, 58: 35–42.

Lane, J. (2008) *Young Children and Racial Justice*. London: National Children's Bureau.

Lee, L. K., K. Douglas and D. Hemenway (2022) 'Crossing Lines – A Change in the Leading Cause of Death among U.S. Children', *New England Journal of Medicine*, 386(16).

Lichtsinn, H., and J. Goldhagen (2023) 'Why the USA Should Ratify the UN Convention on the Rights of the Child', *BMJ Paediatrics Open*, 7(1), pp. e001355.

Liebschner, J. (1992) *A Child's Work*. Cambridge: Lutterworth Press.

Lilley, I. M. (1967) *Friedrich Froebel*. Cambridge: Cambridge University Press.

Louis, D. S. (2008) *Again, Again!: Understanding Schemas in Young Children*. A&C Black.

Louis, D. S. (2022) *Observing Young Children*. Online: Froebel Trust.

Louis, D. S. (2023) *Observing Learning in Early Childhood*. London: SAGE.

Louis, D. S. 'Inspiring Early Learning'. *Froebel Trust Conference 2025*, Sheffield, 29 March 2025.

Louis, D. S., and H. Betteridge (2020) 'Unconscious Bias in the Observation, Assessment and Planning Process', *Foundation Stage Forum*. https://eyfs.info/articles.html/general/unconscious-bias-in-the-observation-assessment-and-planning-process-r338/. (Accessed: 9 August 2025).

Louis, D. S., and H. Betteridge (2024) *Let's Talk About Race in the Early Years*. London: Routledge.

Louv, R. (2008) *Last Child in the Woods: Saving Our Children from Nature Deficit Disorder*. 2nd edn. Chapel Hill NC: Algonquin Books.
Maguire, M. C., and J. Dunn (1997) 'Friendships in Early Childhood, and Social Understanding', *International Journal of Behavioral Development*, 21(4): 669–86.
Malloch, S., and C. Trevarthen (2009) *Communicative Musicality: Exploring the Basis of Human Companionship*. Oxford: Oxford University Press.
Mamidipudi, A., and V. Murthy (2023) 'Raga and the Problem of Ownership: Knowledge and Culture in Carnatic Music', in A. M. Dagmar Schäfer and Marius Buning (eds) *Ownership of Knowledge: Beyond Intellectual Property*. Massachusetts Institute of Technology: The MIT Press, pp. 121–52.
Manjapra, K. (2014) *Age of Entanglement*. Massachusetts: Harvard University Press.
Manning-Morton, J. (2024) *From Birth to Three: An Early Years Educators Handbook*. Oxon: Routledge.
Maslow, A. H. (1943) 'A Theory of Human Motivation', *Psychological Review*, 50, pp. 370–96.
Matsumura, N. (2024) 'Froebelian Researchers and the Implications for Research Practice in Post-Second World War Japan: Two Case Studies of Professor Shoji Masako and Professor Ogasawara Michio', in T. Bruce, Y. Nishida, S. Powell, H. Wasmuth and J. Whinnett (eds) *The Bloomsbury Handbook to Friedrich Froebel*. London: Bloomsbury, p. 451.
May, H., and M. Carr (2015) 'Te Whariki: A Uniquely Woven Curriculum Shaping Policy, Pedagogy and Practice in Aotearoa New Zealand', in Tricia David, Kathy Goouch and S. Powell (eds) *The Routledge International Handbook of Philosophies and Theories of Early Childhood Education and Care*. Oxon: Routledge.
Mayor of London (2023) 'Universal Basic Income Trials'. London Assembly.
Mbolekwa, S. N., and T. Bruce (2024) 'From Freire to Froebel', in T. Bruce, Y. Nishida, S. Powell, H. Wasmuth and J. Whinnett (eds) *The Bloomsbury Handbook to Friedrich Froebel*. London: Bloomsbury, p. 444.
McCormack, M., A. Silke, A. Kearns, L. O'Toole, P. Stafford, T. Stokes and M. Urban (2024) 'Pedagogies of Hope', in

T. Bruce, Y. Nishida, S. Powell, H. Wasmuth and J. Whinnett (eds) *The Bloomsbury Handbook to Friedrich Froebel*. London: Bloomsbury, pp. 328–35.

McCormick, C., and S. McIntosh (2020) 'Tailoring Traditional Tales as Tools for Our Trade: Transforming Literacy in the Early Years', in T. Bruce, McNair Lynn and J. Whinnett (eds) *Putting storytelling at the heart of early childhood practice*. London: Routledge, pp. 31–63.

McDaniel, S. C., D. Mahatmya, and A. L. Bruhn (2024) 'Educator Burnout in the Age of COVID-19: A Mediation Analysis of Perceived Stressors, Work Sense of Coherence, and Sociodemographic Characteristics', *Teaching and Teacher Education*, 137, 104384. https://www.sciencedirect.com/science/article/abs/pii/S0742051X23003724. (Accessed: 1 June 2025).

McGarvey, D. (2022) 'Freedom from Want'. *Reith Lectures*. Glasgow: BBC Radio 4.

McNair, L., and C. Cerdan (2022) 'Nurturing Self-Regulation'. Online: Froebel Trust.

Mignolo, W. (2012) 'Decolonizing Western Epistemology/Building Decolonial Epistemologies', *Decolonizing Epistemologies: Latina/o Theology and Philosophy*, pp. 19–43. Transdisciplinary Theological Colloquia (FUP) (New York, NY, 2011; online edn, Fordham Scholarship Online, 20 September 2012), https://doi.org/10.5422/fordham/9780823241354.003.0002. (Accessed: 9 March 2026).

Moll, L. C., C. Amanti, D. Neff and N. Gonzalez (1992) 'Funds of Knowledge for Teaching: Using a Qualitative Approach to Connect Homes and Classrooms', *Theory Into Practice*, 31(2): 132–41.

Montiel-McCann, C., and M. Julios-Costa (2025) 'A Hostile Environment: Language, Race, Surveillance and the Media'. Online: Runnymede Trust.

Moorhouse, P. (2021) 'The Wonder of Woodwork'. Online: Froebel Trust.

Morgan, J., C. Leeson and R. C. Dillon (2013) 'How Can Schools Support Children with a Parent in Prison?', *Pastoral Care in Education*, 31(3): 199–210.

Murove, M. F. (2020) 'African Traditional Humanism and the Ethic of Collectivism', *African Politics and Ethics*. Cham: Palgrave Macmillan, pp. 103–14.

Murphy, K. (2022) *Supporting the Wellbeing of Children with SEND*. London: Speechmark.
Nair, V. K., W. Farah and I. Cushing (2023) 'A Critical Analysis of Standardized Testing in Speech and Language Therapy', *Language, Speech and Hearing Services in Schools*, 54(3), pp. 781–93.
National Statistics, Office, H. (2024) 'Stop and Search and Arrests: England and Wales, Year ended 31 March 2023': Home Office.
Nauer, R. (October 2023) 'RE: Tour of Keilhau'. Type to Communication, P.
Nazzal, R. (2019) 'The Olive Tree and the Palestinian Struggle against Settler-Colonialism', *Canada and Beyond: A Journal of Canadian Literary and Cultural Studies*, 8: 87–93.
Neumann, K. (2024) 'Peace as Unification of Life – Peace Building as Hidden Curriculum in Froebel's *Education of Man*', in T. Bruce, Y. Nishida, S. Powell, H. Wasmuth and J. Whinnett (eds) *The Bloomsbury Handbook to Friedrich Froebel*. London: Bloomsbury, pp. 87–94.
Ngubane, N. I., and M. Makua (2021a) 'Intersection of Ubuntu Pedagogy and Social Justice: Transforming South African Higher Education', *Transformation in Higher Education*, 6: 1–8.
Ngubane, N. I., and M. Makua (2021b) 'Ubuntu Pedagogy – Transforming Educational Practices in South Africa through an African Philosophy: From Theory to Practice', *Inkanyiso: Journal of Humanities and Social Sciences*, 13(1): 1–12.
Niinimäki, K., G. Peters, H. Dahlbo, P. Perry, T. Rissanen, A. Gwilt, K. Niinimäki, G. Peters, H. Dahlbo, P. Perry, T. Rissanen and A. Gwilt (2020) 'The Environmental Price of Fast Fashion', *Nature Reviews Earth & Environment*, 1(4): 189–200.
Norren, D. E. v. (2023) 'Gross National Happiness in Bhutan: Is Buddhist Constitutionalism Legitimate in the Age of Secularism? A Post-Colonial View', *Religions*, 14(1), pp. 72.
Nuttall, J. (ed.) (2013) *Weaving Te Whariki*. 2nd edn. Wellington: NZCER Press.
OMEP (2025) 'Educating for Peace and Human Rights'. Online: OMEP. Available at: https://omepworld.org/peace-and-human-rights/ (Accessed: 1 May 2025).
Paley, V. (1984) *Boys and Girls: Superheroes in the Doll Corner*. Chicago: University of Chicago Press.

Pascal, C., and T. Bertram (2024) 'Young Voices on Covid-19: An Exploration of the Froebel Storytelling Approach in Support for Young Children's Agency and Autonomy through the Covid-19 Pandemic', in T. Bruce, Y. Nishida, S. Powell, H. Wasmuth and J. Whinnett (eds) *The Bloomsbury Handbook to Friedrich Froebel*. London: Bloomsbury, pp. 460–9.

Pascal, P. C., P. T. Bertram, T. Bruce, H. Lyndon, S. Cave and S. Bennett (2026) *Being and Becoming a Froebelian Community of Evidenced Practice*. London: Routledge.

Pemberton, L. (2025) *Creating Systemic Change: The Animated Resource*. Online: Kinderly. Available at: https://kinderly.co.uk/2025/02/20/creating-systemic-change-the-animated-resource/ (Accessed: 1 June 2025).

Powell, S., and K. Goouch (2019) 'Mother's Songs in Daycare for Babies', in T. Bruce, P. Elfer, S. Powell and L. Werth (eds) *The Routledge International Handbook of Froebel and Early Childhood Practice*. Oxon: Routledge, pp. 154–65.

Pungello, E. P., I. U. Iruka, A. M. Dotterer, R. Mills-Koonce and J. S. Reznick (2009) 'The Effects of Socioeconomic Status, Race, and Parenting on Language Development in Early Childhood', *Dev Psychol*, 45(2), pp. 544–57.

Puntambekar, S. V. (2023) 'The Hindu Concept of Human Freedoms', *The UNESCO Courier*, Available at: UNESCO.

Purvis, B., Y. Mao and D. Robinson (2019) 'Three Pillars of Sustainability: In Search of Conceptual Origins', *Sustainability Science*, 14(3), pp. 681–95.

Quinn, S. M. F., and J. P. Manning (2013) 'Recognising the Ethical Implications of the Use of Photography in Early Childhood Educational Settings', *Contemporary Issues in Early Childhood*, 14(3), pp. 270–8.

Ramirez, J., C. P. Vélez-Zapata and R. Maher (2024) 'Green Colonialism and Decolonial Feminism: A Study of Wayúu Women's Resistance in La Guajira', *Human Relations*, 77(7): 937–64.

Razzall, K. (2024) 'Getting Down and Dirty with Froebel on the Allotment', in T. Bruce, Y. Nishida, S. Powell, H. Wasmuth and J. Whinnett (eds) *The Bloomsbury Handbook to Friedrich Froebel*. London: Bloomsbury, pp. 181–6.

Read, J. (2019) 'Tracing Froebel's Legacy: The Spread of the Kindergarten Movement across Europe and Beyond and His

Influence of Educators', in T. Bruce, P. Elfer, S. Powell and L. Werth (eds) *The Routledge International Handbook of Froebel and Early Childhood Practice*. Oxon: Routledge, pp. 14–18.

Robinson, K. H., and C. J. Diaz (2016) *Diversity and Difference in Childhood: Issues for Theory and Practice*. London: Open University Press.

Robson, S. (2010) 'Self-Regulation and Metacognition in Young Children's Self-Intiated Play and Reflective Dialogue', *International Journal of Early Years Education*, 18(3), pp. 227–41.

Roosevelt, E. (2012) *Tomorrow Is Now*. London: Penguin.

Roosevelt, F. (1941) The Four Freedoms Speech.

Rosen, M. (2024) 'Michael Rosen Day'. Available at: https://www.michaelrosen.co.uk/michaelrosenday/ (Accessed: 29 July 2025).

Rosen, M., and A. Young (2015) *What Is Humanism? How Do You Live Without a God? And Other Big Questions for Kids*. London: Wayland.

Rowland, A. (n.d.) *POSIE Study*: Oxford Brookes University. Available at: https://www.posie-study.co.uk/home (Accessed: 1 June 2025).

Sachs, A. (2003) 'The Ultimate "Other": Post-Colonialism and Alexander von Humboldt's Ecological Relationship with Nature', *History and Theory*, 42(4): 111–35.

Sakr, M. (2024) *Rights-Based Learning and Care in the Baby Room*. London: Online https://babyrooms-inspiringleaders.co.uk/. (Accessed: 14 February 2025).

Sakr, M., and Kaur, V. (2024) 'Re-Imagining the Froebelian Influence on Early Childhood Education as a Dynamic and Ever-Changing Web of Encounter', *Pedagogy, Culture & Society*, 32(4), pp. 923–40.

Sandy Hook Promise (2025) '17 Facts about Gun Violence and School Shooting'. Sandy Hook Promise. Available at: https://www.sandyhookpromise.org/blog/gun-violence/facts-about-gun-violence-and-school-shootings/ (Accessed: 8 April 2025).

Schamberger, I. (2024) 'A Discussion of Froebel from Authentic to Modern', in T. Bruce, Y. Nishida, S. Powell, H. Wasmuth and J. Whinnett(eds) *The Bloomsbury Handbook to Friedrich Froebel*. London: Bloomsbury, pp. 311–18.

Scottish Government, Education Scotland (2020) 'Realising the Ambition'. Scotland: Education Scotland.

Scottish Government, Cabinet Secretary for Social Justice, M.f.E., Cabinet Secretary for Education and Skills (2024) 'Children's Rights'. https://www.gov.scot/policies/human-rights/childrens-rights/. (Accessed: 13 March 2025): Scottish Government.

Sherrington, T., and Stafford, S. (2018) 'Say It Again, Better: Setting High Expectations by Asking Students to Re-Frame Their Inital answers'. Available at: https://my.chartered.college/research-hub/say-it-again-better-setting-high-expectations-by-asking-students-to-re-frame-their-initial-answers/ 2025. (Accessed: 9 August 2025).

Social Justice Collective (n.d.) 'Social Justice Collective'. Online. Available at: https://socialjusticecollective.co.uk/language (Accessed: 25 July 2025).

Sroufe, L. A. (1977) 'Wariness of Strangers and the Study of Infant Development', *Child Development*, 48(3), pp. 731–46.

Sullivan, R. (2001) 'Rethinking Christianity in Enlightened Europe', *Eighteenth-Century Studies*, 34(2), pp. 289–309.

Tang, F., S. Guimarães and C. Rubiano (2025) 'Introduction', in F. Tang, S. Guimarães and C. Rubiano (eds) *Young Children's Identities*. London: Routledge, pp. 1–14.

Tang, F., and C. Rubiano (2025) *Young Children's Identities*. London: Routledge.

Tang, F., and J. Zhao (2024) 'Spirituality in Early Childhood: A Froebelian Lens on the Role of Women in a Chinese Context', in T. Bruce Y. Nishida, S. Powell, H. Wasmuth and J. Whinnett (eds) *The Bloomsbury Handbook to Friedrich Froebel*. London: Bloomsbury, pp. 311–18.

Taylor, A. (2013) *Reconfiguring the Natures of Childhood.* Contesting Early childhood Oxon: Routledge.

Tembo, S., M. Dujczynski and M. Sakr (2025) '"Maybe That Makes a Difference Actually": Attuning to Praxis for Anti-Racist Social Justice Leadership among Nursery School Head Teachers in the UK', *Journal of Early Childhood Research*, 23(1): 31–45.

Tembo, S. B., Simon (2024) 'Liminal Relationalities: On Collaborative Writing With/in and Against Race in the Study of Early Childhood', *International Journal of Qualitative Studies in Education*, 37(2), pp. 530–44.

Thomas, N., and D. Stoecklin (2018) 'Recognition and Capability – A new Way to Understand How Children Can Achieve Their Rights?', ?. In C. Baraldi and T. Cockburn (eds) *Theorising*

Childhood: Citizenship, Rights and Participation, Studies in Childhood and Youth. Cham: Palgrave Macmillan, pp. 73–94.

Titley, A. (2023) *'Deferred, Denied, and Dying Dreams': The Experiences of Minoritized Ethnic Prospective Pre-Service Teacher Candidates in Ireland*. Dublin City University.

Toval, C. A., S. M. Darivemula, T. D. Wilson, J. L. Conklin and O. M. Young (2024) 'Interventions to Mitigate Pregnancy-Related Mortality and Morbidity in Black Birthing People: A Systematic Review', *American Journal of Obstetrics & Gynecology MFM*, 6(10). https://www.sciencedirect.com/science/article/abs/pii/S2589933324001903. (Accessed: 8 April 2025).

Tovey, H. (2007) *Playing Outdoors: Spaces and Places, Risk and Challenge. Debating Play* Berkshire: McGraw-Hill.

Tovey, H. (2017) *Bringing the Froebel Approach to Your Early Years Practice. Bringing... to Your Early Years Practice*. London: Routledge.

Tovey, H. (2020) 'Froebel's Principles and Practice Today'. Online: Froebel Trust.

Tovey, H. (2022) 'An Introduction to Froebel, Children and Nature'. Online: Froebel Trust.

Trevarthen, C. (2013) 'What Young Children Know about Living and Learning with Companions', *Nordic Early Childhood Education Research*, 6, pp. 1–9.

Trevarthen, C., and K. J. Aitken (2001) 'Infant Intersubjectivity: Research, Theory and Clinical Applications', *Journal of Child Psychology*, 42(1), pp. 1–48.

Tweneboa, K. (2024) *Our Country in Crisis*. London: Orion.

UK Government, Department for Education (2024) 'School Uniforms: Guidance for Schools'. gov.uk.

UNESCO (2008) 'Manden Charter, Proclaimed in Kurukan Fuga'. Available at: https://ich.unesco.org/en/RL/manden-charter-proclaimed-in-kurukan-fuga-00290?RL=00290 (Accessed: 6 June 2024).

UNICEF (1989) The United Nations Convention on the Rights of the Child.

UNICEF (2025) 'History of Child Rights', UNICEF. Available at: https://www.unicef.org/child-rights-convention/history-child-rights (Accessed: 12 July 2025).

United Nations 'Understanding Hate Speech'. Available at: https://www.un.org/en/hate-speech/understanding-hate-speech/hate-speech-versus-freedom-of-speech (Accessed: 3 May 2025).

United Nations (1948) *Universal Declaration of Human Rights*. Online https://www.un.org/en/about-us/universal-declaration-of-human-rights (Accessed 2 March 2026).

United Nations (2012) 'The Rabat Plan of Action'. Online: United Nations Human Rights.

United Nations (2015) 'Sustainable Development Goals' Online: United Nations Department of Economic and Social Affairs Sustainable Development.

United Nations Educational Scientific Cultural Organization and United Nations Children's Fund (2024) 'Global Report on Early Childhood Care and Education: The Right to a Strong Foundation'. France: UNESCO, UNICEF.

Unity in Diversity (2025) Directed by Froebel Trust.

University of Washington Tacoma (2015) 'Diversity and Social Justice Glossary'. Available at: https://www.tacoma.uw.edu/sites/default/files/2021-03/diversity_glossary.pdf.pdf (Accessed: 23 December 2024).

Veer, L., and Dezentje, A. (2023) 'UNESCO Courier'. Available at: https://courier.unesco.org/en/articles/human-rights-and-cultural-perspectives (Accessed: 2 May 2025).

Vygotsky (1978) *Mind in Society*. Massachusetts: Harvard University Press.

Wall, I. r. (2024) 'The Right to Protest', *The International Journal of Human Rights*, 28(8–9): 1378–93.

Warneken, F., and Tomasello, M. (2014) 'Extrinsic Rewards Undermine Altruistic Tendencies in 20-Month-Olds', *Motivation Science*, 1(S), pp. 43–8.

Welsh Government (2022) 'Curriculum for Wales'. Online: Welsh Government.

Whalley, M. (2017) *Involving Parents in Their Children's Learning*. London: Sage.

Whinnett, J. (2020) *Froebel's Gifts and Block Play Today*.

Whinnett, J. (2024) 'Editor's Introduction', in T. Bruce, Y. Nishida, S. Powell, H. Wasmuth and J. Whinnett (eds) *The Bloomsbury Handbook to Friedrich Froebel*. London: Bloomsbury, p. 175.

Whinnett, J. (2025) 'A Froebelian Path in Bewildering Times'. *Froebel Trust Conference*, Online: Froebel Trust.

Whinnett, J., T. Bruce and L. McNair (2020) *Putting Storytelling at the Heart of Early Childhood Practice*. London: Routledge.

Whistler, E. M., and L. Montgomery (2024) 'Supporting Children with Additional Needs'. Online: Froebel Trust.

Whitebread, Penny Coltman, Deborah Pino Pasternak, Claire Sangster, Valeska Grau, Sue Bingham, Qais Almeqdad and D. Demetriou (2008) 'The Development of Two Observational Tools for Assessing Metacognition and Self-Regulated Learning in Young Children', *Metacognition Learning*, 4, pp. 63–85.

Whitehead, M. R. (2009) *Supporting Language And Literacy Development in the Early Years.* Supporting Early Learning. 2nd edn. Berkshire: McGraw-Hill Education.

Whitehead, M. R. (2010) *Language & Literacy in the Early Years 0–7* London: Sage. Available at: http://digital.casalini.it/978144 6203354. (Accessed: 9 July 2025).

Wilkin, K., C. Thornton and G. Allen-Baker (2025) 'Teacher-Led Yoga/Mindfulness in the Key Stage 1 Classroom. Survey of Educators across North-East England', *Early Childhood Education Journal*, 54: 985–96.

Williams, G. (2003) 'Encyclopedia of Exploration to 1800: A Comprehensive Reference Guide to the History and Literature of Exploration, Travel and Colonization from the Earliest Times to the Year 1800', *The Journal of Imperial and Commonwealth History*, 31(3), pp. 114–75.

Williams, H., and R. Joshi (2025) 'Connecting with Families and Communities'. Online: Froebel Trust.

Winnicott, D. W. (1960) 'The Theory of the Parent-Infant Relationship', *International Journal of Psychoanalysis*, 41(6), pp. 585–95.

Wolfe, P. (2006) 'Settler Colonialism and the Elimination of the Native', *Journal of Genocide Research*, 8(4): 387–409.

Wolff, K., and A. Stapp (2019) 'Investigating Early Childhood Teachers' Perceptions of a Preschool Yoga Program', *SAGE Open*, 9(1). https://journals.sagepub.com/doi/full/10.1177/21582 44018821758. (Accessed: 19 July 2025).

Women and Equalities Committee, Report, H.o.C.C. (2023) 'Black Maternal Health'. UK parliment.

Worley, M., and N. Copsey (2016) 'White Youth: The Far Right, Punk and British Youth Culture, 1977–87', *JOMEC Journal*, (9): 27–47.

Wulf, A. (2023) *Magnificent Rebels: The First Romantics and the Invention of the Self*. London: John Murray.

Wyse, D. and C. Hacking (2024) *The Balancing Act*. London: Routledge.

Xu, Y. (2021) 'Challenging Gender Stereotypes through Gender-Sensitive Practices in Early Years Education and Care', *Early Education Journal*, 93, pp. 10–12.

Xu, Y. and A. Xie (2021) 'A Study of the Deep Differences between Eastern and Western Philosophies in Ideological and Political Education', *Advances in Social Sciences, Education and Humanities Research*, 575, pp. 285–92.

Yılmaz, A. D. (2025) 'Teaching on the Margins: What Do Preschool Teachers Need to Support Refugee Children?', *EECERA 2025 Conference – Guest Blog #1*. Available at: https://www.linkedin.com/pulse/eecera-2025-conference-guest-blog-1-sw5ff/ 2025. (Accessed: 28 July 2025).

Yoon, H. (2023) 'Introduction', *Reimagining Diversity, Equity, and Justice in Early Childhood*. New York: Routledge, pp. 2–20.

Young, B. L. (2024) *Eight Weeks: Looking Back, Moving Forwards, Defying the Odds*. London: Penguin.

INDEX